THE COMPLETE BOOK OF
ALPHABET

AMERICAN
EDUCATION
PUBLISHING™

Columbus, Ohio

Copyright © 2004 School Specialty Publishing. Published by American Education Publishing™, an imprint of School Specialty Publishing, a member of the School Specialty Family.

Printed in the United States of America. All rights reserved. Except as permitted under the United States Copyright Act, no part of this publication may be reproduced or distributed in any form or by any means, or stored in a database or retrieval system, without prior written permission from the publisher, unless otherwise indicated.

Send all inquiries to:
School Specialty Publishing
8720 Orion Place
Columbus, OH 43240-2111

ISBN 1-57768-603-9

9 10 11 12 13 14 COU 11 10 09 08 07 06

Table of Contents

Letter Recognition A-Z

Letter Aa 6-9
Letter Bb 10-14
Letter Cc 15-19
Letter Dd 20-24
Letter Ee 25-28
Letter Ff 29-33
Review Letters Aa-Ff 34-40
Letter Gg 41-45
Letter Hh 46-50
Letter Ii 51-54
Letter Jj 55-59
Review Letters Aa-Jj 60-66
Letter Kk 67-71
Letter Ll 72-76
Letter Mm 77-81
Letter Nn 82-86
Letter Oo 87-91
Review Letters Aa-Oo . . 92-97
Letter Pp 98-102
Letter Qq 103-107
Letter Rr 108-112
Letter Ss 113-117
Letter Tt 118-122
Review Letters Aa-Tt . . 123-131
Letter Uu 132-135
Letter Vv 136-140
Letter Ww 141-145
Letter Xx 146-149
Letter Yy 150-154

Letter Zz 155-158
Review Letters Aa-Zz . 159-182

Letter Sounds A-Z

Vowel Aa 184
Beginning Consonant Bb . 185
Beginning Consonant Cc . 186
Beginning Sounds
   Aa, Bb, Cc 187
Beginning Consonant Dd . 188
Vowel Ee 189
Beginning Consonant Ff . . 190
Beginning Sounds
   Dd, Ee, Ff 191
Beginning Consonant Gg . 192
Beginning Consonant Hh . 193
Beginning Sounds
   Ff, Gg, Hh 194
Vowel Ii 195
Beginning Sounds
   Gg, Hh, Ii 196
Beginning Consonant Jj . . 197
Beginning Consonant Kk . . 198
Beginning Consonant Ll . . 199
Beginning Sounds Jj, Kk, Ll . . 200
Beginning Consonant Mm . 201
Beginning Consonant Nn . 202
Vowel Oo 203
Beginning Sounds
   Mm, Nn, Oo 204

Beginning Consonant Pp . 205
Beginning Sounds
  Mm, Nn, Pp 206
Beginning Consonant Qq . 207
Beginning Consonant Rr . . 208
Beginning Sounds
  Pp, Qq, Rr 209
Beginning Consonant Ss . . 210
Beginning Sounds
  Qq, Rr, Ss 211
Beginning Consonant Tt . . 212
Vowel Uu 213
Beginning Sounds
  Ss, Tt, Uu 214
Beginning Consonant Vv . 215
Beginning Consonant Ww . 216
Beginning Sounds
  Tt, Vv, Ww 217
Consonant Xx 218
Beginning Sounds
  Vv, Ww, Xx 219
Beginning Consonant Yy . 220
Beginning Consonant Zz . . 221
Beginning Sounds
  Xx, Yy, Zz 222
Beginning Sounds Yy, Zz . . 223
Review Letters Aa-Zz 224
Ending Consonant
  Sounds 225-227
Beginning and Ending
  Consonants 228-229
Short Vowels 230

Review Short Vowels Aa, Ii . 231
Review Short Vowels Aa, Ii,
  Oo, Uu, Ee 232
Vowel Sounds 233
Long Vowels 234
Review Long Vowels 235
Short and Long Vowels . . . 236
Words With a 237
Words With e 238
Words With i 239
Words With o 240
Words With u 241
Review Short and
  Long Vowels 242
My Vowel List 243
Super Silent e 244
Consonant Blends . . . 245-246
Ending Consonant
  Blends 247-248
Rhyming Words 249-252

**Printing Letters and
Words A-Z**
Aa-Zz 254-306

**Songs, Rhymes, and Activities
for Every Letter A-Z**
Aa-Zz 309-335

Answer Key 336-352

Name _____

Letter A Uppercase

✏ **Trace** the letters.

A A A A A A

A A A A A

Letter a Lowercase

✏ **Trace** the letters.

a a a a a

a a a a a

These pictures begin with the letter **Aa**. 🖍 **Color** the pictures.

Name _____

Letter Aa

✏️ **Circle** the **A** or **a** in these words:

apple	alligator	angel	bat
Amy	dance	Andy	art
ambulance	draw	teacher	nap

The letter **Aa** can have more than one sound. ✏️ **Circle** the pictures that start with the sound of **Aa**. 🖍️ **Color** the pictures.

7

Letter Recognition

Name _____

These words start with **A** or **a**.

✏ **Write** the **lowercase a** on the line.
Color the pictures. 🖍

A is for _____pple.

A is for _____ngel.

A is for _____nt.

Letter
Aa

Name _____

You can help the 🧑‍🚀 find the 🚀.

✏️ **Draw** a line to follow the letters **A** and **a**.
Color the picture. 🖍️

a c C B

A a a A a A C

A A a A b

a C b B

A c

a b

A

a

A a a A

Letter Recognition

Name _____

Letter B Uppercase

Trace the letters.

B B B B B

B B B B B

Letter b Lowercase

Trace the letters.

b b b b b

b b b b b

These pictures begin with the letter **Bb**. **Color** the pictures.

Name _____

Letter Bb

Circle the **B** or **b** in these words:

Bill	brown	doll	Bonnie
boy	baby	balloon	pig
bat	book	butter	band

Circle the pictures that start with the sound of **Bb**.
Color the pictures.

Letter Recognition

Name _____

These words start with **B** or **b**.

Write the **lowercase b** on the line.
Color the pictures.

B is for _____uttons.

B is for _____at.

B is for _____ug.

Name _____

Letter Bb

Bobby Bear blows beautiful bubbles.

Color the bubbles with pictures that begin with the sound of **Bb**.

Letter Recognition

Letter

Find each hidden **B** and **b**.

Draw a **blue** circle around each **B** and a **green** circle around each **b**.

Name _____

Letter C Uppercase

✎ **Trace** the letters.

C · C · C · C · C · C

C · C · C · C · C

Letter C Lowercase

✎ **Trace** the letters.

c · c · c · c · c

c · c · c · c · c

These pictures begin with the letter **Cc**. 🖍 **Color** the pictures.

Letter Recognition

Name _____

Letter Cc

✏️ **Circle** the **C** or **c** in these words:

cat   Casey   ran   can

cow   corn   cup   Carol

hand   wall   crack   car

✏️ **Circle** the pictures that start with the sound of **Cc** .
Color the pictures.

Name _____

These words start with **C** or **c**.

Write the **lowercase c** on the line.
Color the pictures.

C is for _____ow.

C is for _____up.

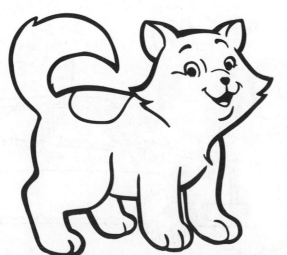

C is for _____at.

17

Name _____

Letter Cc

Help Calico Cat catch what she is chasing.

Circle the pictures that begin with the sound of **Cc**. **Color** the pictures.

Letter Recognition

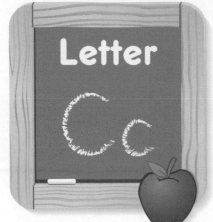

Letter Cc

Name _____

Find each **C** and **c** that the cat has made with the yarn.

Color the **UPPERCASE C's red. Color** the **lowercase c's** yellow.

Letter Recognition

Name _____

Letter D Uppercase

✎ **Trace** the letters.

D   D D D D D

D D D D D

Letter d Lowercase

✎ **Trace** the letters.

d   d d d d

d d d d d

These pictures begin with the letter **Dd**. 🖍 **Color** the pictures.

Letter Dd

Circle the **D** or **d** in these words:

doll	Darcy	desk	big
door	David	jump	dog
pig	Daddy	duck	Debbie

Circle the pictures that start with the sound of **Dd**.
Color the pictures.

These words start with **D** or **d**.

Write the **lowercase d** on the line.
Color the pictures.

D is for _____og.

D is for _____rum.

D is for _____uck.

Name _____

Help Danny Duck find his way to the pond.

Color the pictures that begin with the sound of **Dd**.

DUCK POND RD.

23

Letter Recognition

Letter Dd

Name _____

Color the spaces with the letters **D** or **d** **purple**. **Color** the spaces with the other letters **orange**.

What did you find?

Color the doll, too!

Name _____

Letter E Uppercase

Trace the letters.

E

Letter e Lowercase

Trace the letters.

e

These pictures begin with the letter **Ee**. Color the pictures.

25

Letter Recognition

Letter Ee

Circle the **E** or **e** in these words:

ear	Elizabeth	his	eleven
dog	house	earth	Eric
ball	elf	cat	envelope

The letter **Ee** can have more than one sound. Circle the pictures that start with the sound of **Ee**. Color the pictures.

Name _____

These words start with **E** or **e**.

Write the **lowercase e** on the line.
Color the pictures.

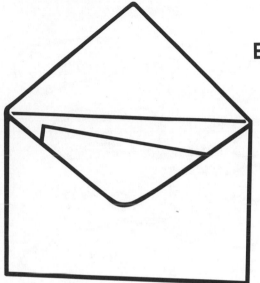

E is for _____nvelope.

E is for _____ggs.

E is for _____lephant.

Name _____

Letter
Ee

Help the 🐘 find its way to the circus tent.

Color the ⬤s with **E** or **e** brown.
Color the other ⬤s green. **Color** the rest of the picture.

Letter F Uppercase

Trace the letters.

Letter f Lowercase

Trace the letters.

These pictures begin with the letter **Ff**. **Color** the pictures.

29

Letter Ff

Name _____

✏️ **Circle** the **F** or **f** in these words:

fire	Faye	took	fork
table	Fred	car	farm
Father	ten	four	fish

✏️ **Circle** the pictures that start with the sound of **Ff**.
Color the pictures. 🖍️

Name _____

These words start with **F** or **f**.

Write the **lowercase f** on the line.
Color the pictures.

F is for _____rog.

F is for _____ish.

F is for _____an.

Letter Recognition

Letter

Name _____

Help the firefighter find each **F** and **f**.

Color a **blue** ⬛ of water around each **F**. **Color** a **green** ⬛ of water around each **f**. **Color** the picture.

A   f   F   c
   d   b   F   f
          e
      F   d
   F   f
          f   F
f   f   F
   F   c
A   d   b   F
          e   f
f   C
   F   f
          F

Name _____

Letter Ff

✏️ **Color** each picture on the fence that begins with the sound of **Ff**.

33

Letter Recognition

Review A-F

Name _____

Practice **writing** the letters **Aa-Ff** by **tracing** the **UPPER** and **lowercase** letters below.

Aa Aa Aa Aa

Bb Bb Bb Bb

Cc Cc Cc Cc

Dd Dd Dd Dd

Ee Ee Ee Ee

Ff Ff Ff Ff

Review
A-F

Name _____

Trace the letters **Aa-Ff**. Then practice **writing** them on the lines below.

Aa

Bb

Cc

Dd

Ee

Ff

Review A-F

Name _____

 **Draw** a line to connect the **UPPER** and **lowercase** letters that belong together.

A

B

a

C

b

c

Review
A-F

Name _____

Draw a line to connect the **UPPER** and **lowercase** letters that belong together.

f

E

d

D

F

e

Review Letters A-F

Name _____

Alphabet Dot-to-Dot

Connect the dots as you say the alphabet, starting with the letter **A**.

Color the picture.

C ● ● D

Cody

B ● ● E

A ● ● F

Name _____

Review

A-F

Match the **UPPER** and **lowercase** letters.

Match beginning sounds with pictures.

 Trace the letters. **Color** the pictures.

 Draw a line from the **UPPERCASE** letter to the picture that starts with that sound. Then **draw** a line to the **lowercase** letter that matches it.

A

b

B

d

Nn Oo Pp Qq Rr Ss Tt

Name _____

C

D

E

F

e

f

c

d

Letter G Uppercase

✏️ **Trace** the letters.

G G G G G

G G G G G

Letter g Lowercase

✏️ **Trace** the letters.

g g g g g

g g g g g

These pictures begin with the letter **Gg**. 🖍️ **Color** the pictures.

Letter Recognition

Letter Gg

Name _____

 **Circle** the **G** or **g** in these words:

goat	Gregory	park	gate
great	tree	Gloria	gift
goose	garden	Georgia	gym

The letter **Gg** can have more than one sound. **Circle** the pictures that start with the sound of **Gg**. **Color** the pictures.

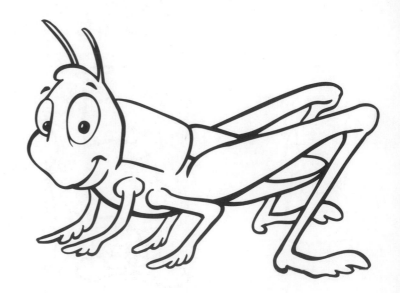

Name _____

These words start with **G** or **g**.

Write the **lowercase g** on the line.
Color the pictures.

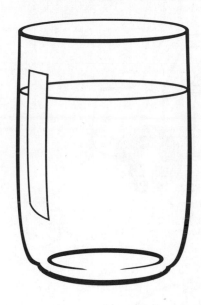

G is for _____lass.

G is for _____ift.

G is for _____irl.

43

Letter Recognition

Name _____

Letter Gg

Which cars need gas?

Draw a line from the gas pump to each car that has a driver that begins with **G** or **g**. **Color** the picture.

GAS

Letter Recognition

44

Letter Gg

Look at each sign in the garden.

Trace each **G** and **g**. Then **color** each sign with **G red** and **g blue**.

How many?

I have

____ G's

____ g's

Letter Recognition

Name _____

Letter [H] Uppercase

✏️ **Trace** the letters.

Letter [h] Lowercase

✏️ **Trace** the letters.

These pictures begin with the letter **Hh**. 🖍️ **Color** the pictures.

Letter Hh

Circle the **H** or **h** in these words:

Heather	hose	house	Ben
Henry	horse	Amy	fat
hand	heart	hat	help

Circle the pictures that start with the sound of **Hh**.
Color the pictures.

Letter Recognition

These words start with **H** or **h**.

Write the **lowercase h** on the line.
Color the pictures.

H is for _____elicopter.

H is for _____orn.

H is for _____at.

Letter **Hh**

Name _____

How many pictures can you find that begin with the sound of **Hh**?

Circle them! **Color** the picture!

HONEY

49

Letter Hh

Name _____

Color the spaces with the **UPPERCASE H** red. Color the spaces with the **lowercase h** purple.

What did you find?

Name _____

Letter I Uppercase

Trace the letters.

Letter i Lowercase

Trace the letters.

These pictures begin with the letter **Ii**. **Color** the pictures.

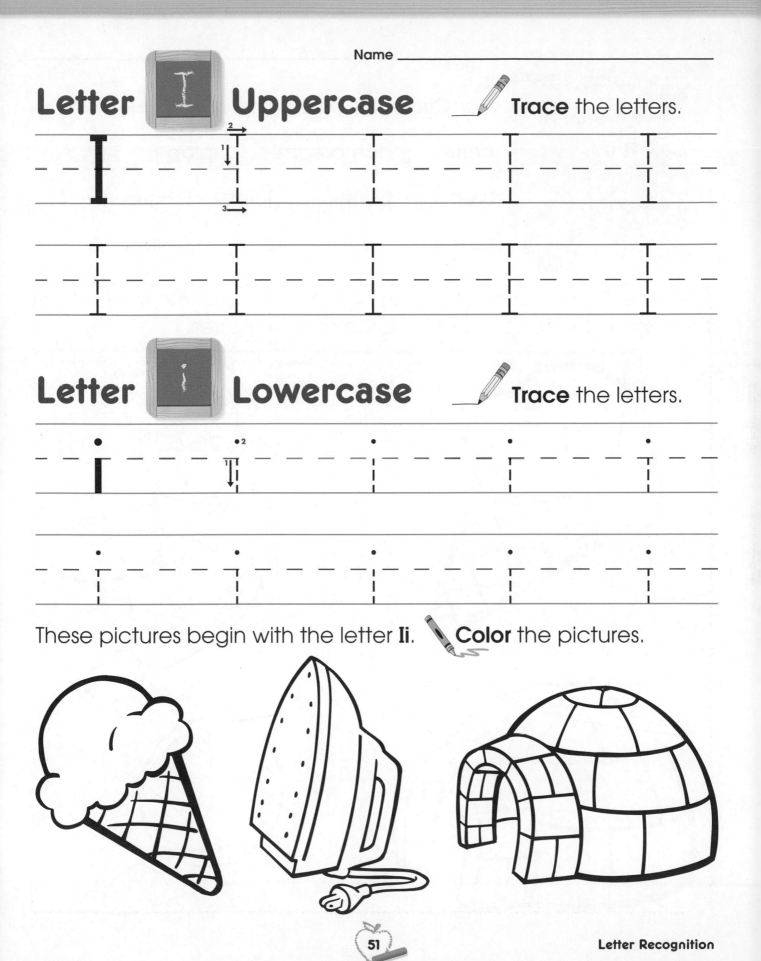

Letter Recognition

Name _____

Letter

Circle the **I** or **i** in these words:

Irene   ice cream   igloo   is

Ivan   home   icing   green

flower   cat   ice   Indian

The letter **Ii** can have more than one sound. **Circle** the pictures that start with the sound of **Ii**. **Color** the pictures.

Name _____

These words start with **I** or **i**.

Write the **lowercase i** on the line.
Color the pictures.

I is for _____nsects.

I is for _____gloo.

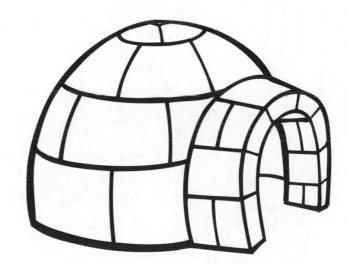

1   **2**

inch

I is for _____nch.

Name _____

Letter
Ii

Help read the 🪶's smoke signals.

Color each **I** **red**. **Color** each **i** **blue**.
Color the rest of the picture!

Name _____

Letter J Uppercase ✏ Trace the letters.

J

Letter j Lowercase ✏ Trace the letters.

j

These pictures begin with the letter **Jj**. 🖍 **Color** the pictures.

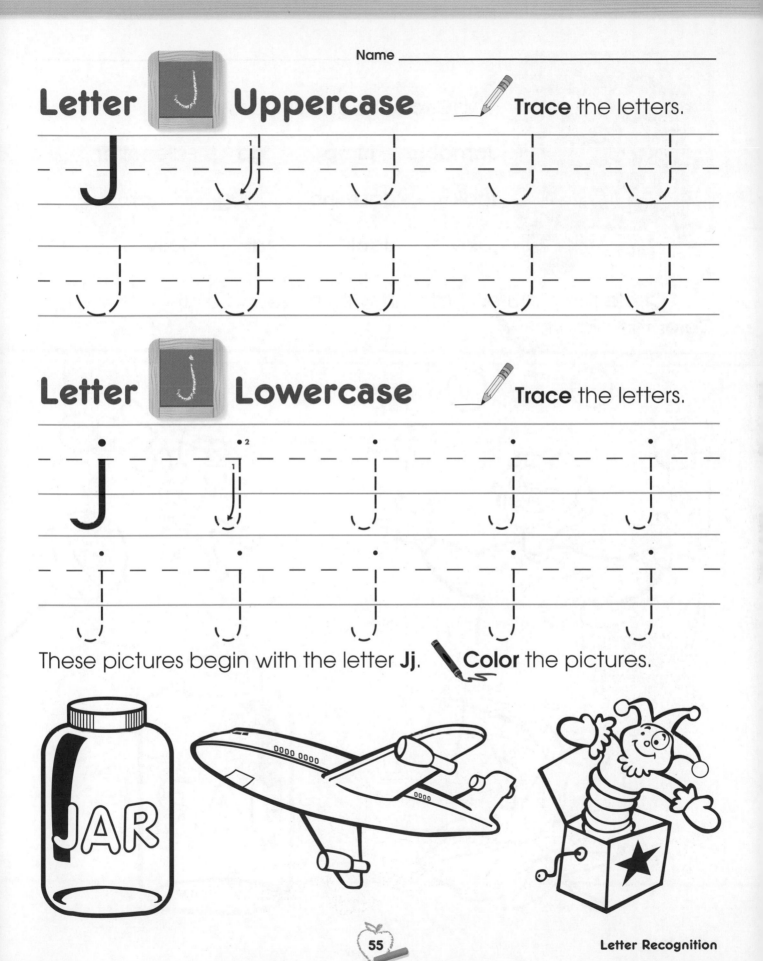

JAR

Letter Recognition

Name _____

Letter

✏ **Circle** the **J** or **j** in these words:

Jamal	jump	go	Jennifer
took	Jasmine	jug	jar
joke	Jack	leaf	jelly

✏ **Circle** the pictures that start with the sound of **Jj**.
Color the pictures.

JAR

Name _____

These words start with **J** or **j**.

Write the **lowercase j** on the line.
Color the pictures.

J is for _____ump rope.

J is for _____ar of _____am.

J is for _____ug.

Letter Recognition

Letter

Jj

Name _____

Jake Jaguar likes jellybeans!

Draw a line from Jake Jaguar to each jellybean that has a picture that begins with the sound of **Jj**. **Color** the pictures with bright colors!

Name _____

Letter

Can you find each hidden **J** and **j** in the picture?

Color each **J red**. **Color** each **j green**. Then **color** the rest of the picture!

Letter Recognition

Name _____

Practice **writing** the letters **Aa-Jj** by **tracing** the **UPPER** and **lowercase** letters below.

Aa   Bb   Cc

Dd   Ee   Ff   Gg

Hh   Ii   Jj

Aa   Bb   Cc

Dd   Ee   Ff   Gg

Hh   Ii   Jj

Review Letters A-J

Review

Name _____

Trace the letters **Aa-Jj**. Then practice **writing** them on the lines below.

Aa   Bb   Cc

Dd   Ee   Ff   Gg

Hh   Ii   Jj

Review Letters A-J

Review A-J

Name _____

 **Draw** a line to connect the **UPPER** and **lowercase** letters that belong together.

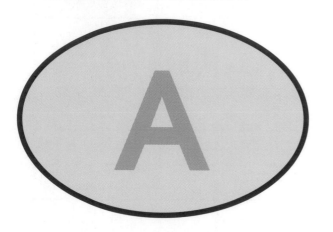

A

C

b

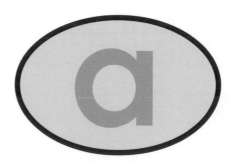

a

c

B

Name _____

Draw a line to connect the **UPPER** and **lowercase** letters that belong together.

e

f

J

F

j

E

Review Letters A-J

Review A-J

Name _____

Draw a line to connect the **UPPER** and **lowercase** letters that belong together.

h

G

g

I

i

H

Name _____

Review

What belongs on the **A, B,** and **C** trees?

Color the pictures that are on the correct letter tree. **Color** the rest of the picture.

65

Start with the letter **a** and connect the dots as you say the alphabet. **Color** the picture.

Name _____

Letter K Uppercase

✏️ **Trace** the letters.

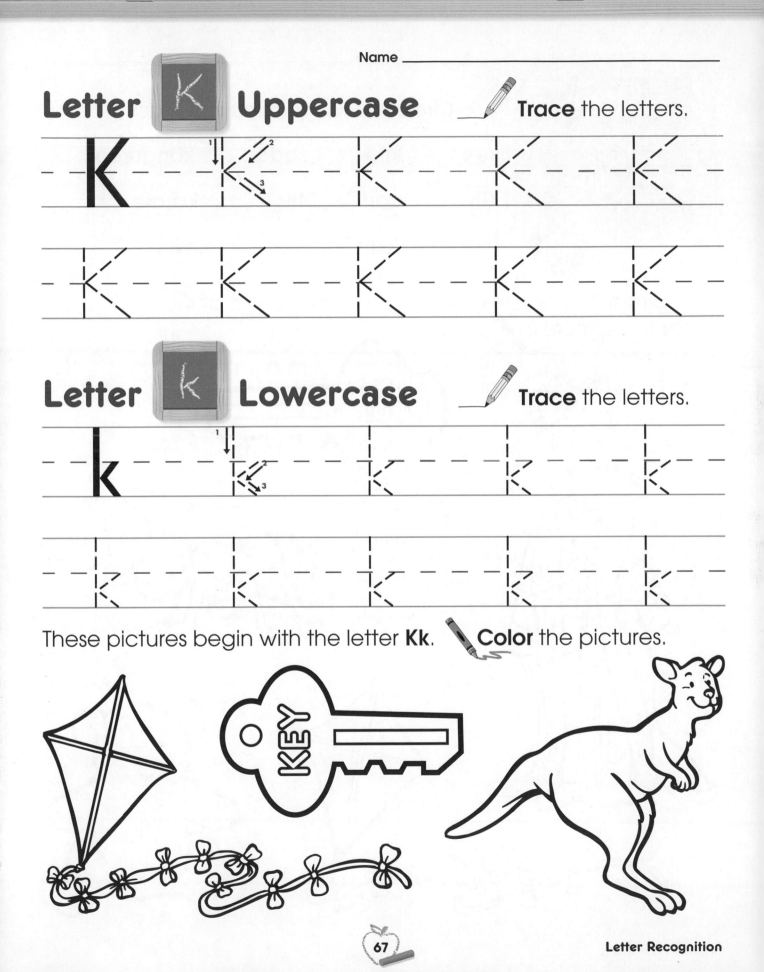

Letter k Lowercase

✏️ **Trace** the letters.

These pictures begin with the letter **Kk**. 🖍️ **Color** the pictures.

Letter Recognition

Name _____

Letter **Kk**

✏️ **Circle** the **K** or **k** in these words:

key	kite	soda	kangaroo
Kim	cart	high	karate
toe	Kelly	art	Kevin

✏️ **Circle** the pictures that start with the sound of **Kk**.
Color the pictures.

Name _____

These words start with **K** or **k**.

✏️ **Write** the **lowercase k** on the line.
Color the pictures. 🖍️

K is for _____angaroo.

K is for _____ing.

K is for _____eg.

 69

Letter Kk

Color each space **brown** that has a picture in it that begins with the sound of **Kk**. **Color** the other spaces **green** to see what hops, jumps, and kicks.

Name _____

Look at each letter on the kites.

Match the letters on the sections of the kites and **color** them the correct colors. Then **color** the rest of the picture.

K = blue
k = yellow

K = yellow
k = red

K = orange
k = purple

K = green
k = red

Letter Recognition

Name _____

Letter L Uppercase

✏ **Trace** the letters.

L

Letter l Lowercase

✏ **Trace** the letters.

l

These pictures begin with the letter **Ll**. 🖍 **Color** the pictures.

Name _____

Letter
Ll

Circle the **L** or **l** in these words:

letter	Larry	lion	Leah
lamp	ladder	book	net
leaf	television	leap	lap

Circle the pictures that start with the sound of **Ll**.
Color the pictures.

Letter Recognition

These words start with **L** or **l**.

Write the **lowercase l** on the line.
Color the pictures.

L is for _____amp.

L is for _____ock.

L is for _____emons.

Letter Recognition

Letter Ll

Lucy lost her luggage! Help her find it.

Color the pictures on the luggage that begin with the sound of **Ll**. Then **color** Lucy's clothes!

luggage

Letter Recognition

Name _____

Letter Ll

It is fun to rake the fall leaves!

Color the leaves with **L** orange. **Color** the leaves with **l** red.

Letter M Uppercase

Trace the letters.

M M M M M M M

M M M M M M

Letter m Lowercase

Trace the letters.

m m m m m m

m m m m m

These pictures begin with the letter **Mm**. **Color** the pictures.

MILK MILK

Letter Recognition

Letter Mm

Name _____

Circle the **M** or **m** in these words:

man	monkey	nest	Maria
spider	hat	flower	mask
make	bird	Martin	Mark

Circle the pictures that start with the sound of **Mm**.
Color the pictures.

Name _____

These words start with **M** or **m**.

Write the **lowercase m** on the line.
Color the pictures.

M is for _____onkey.

M is for _____ittens.

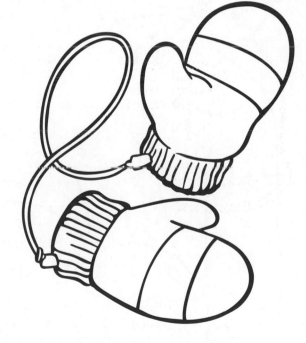

M is for _____oon.

79

Letter Recognition

Name _____

Letter Mm

You can help the find the cheese.

Draw a **green** line to follow each **M** and **m**.

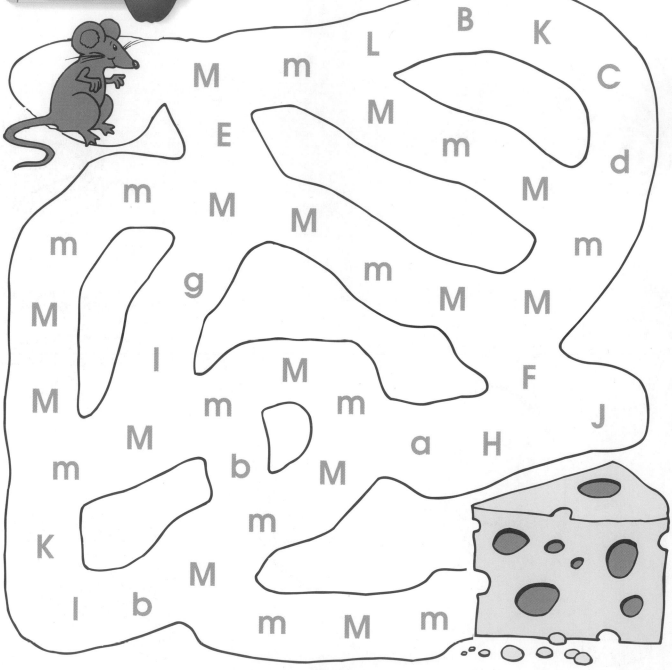

Letter Mm

Name _____

 **Draw a line** from each  to a picture that begins with the sound of **Mm**.
Color the pictures.

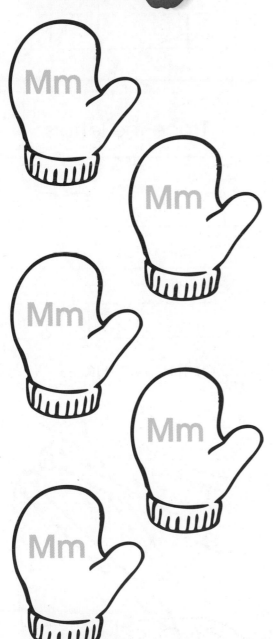

Mm
Mm
Mm
Mm
Mm

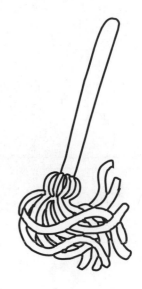

MILK MILK

PENCIL

Letter Recognition

Letter N Uppercase

Trace the letters.

N N N N N N

N N N N N

Letter n Lowercase

Trace the letters.

n n n n n

n n n n n

These pictures begin with the letter **Nn**. **Color** the pictures.

Name _____

Letter Nn

Circle the **N** or **n** in these words:

Nathan   man   net   nine

under   ball   no   nest

Mary   Nancy   nails   never

Circle the pictures that start with the sound of **Nn**.
Color the pictures.

83

Letter Recognition

Name _____

These words start with **N** or **n**.

_____ **Write** the **lowercase n** on the line.
Color the pictures.

N is for _____est.

N is for _____uts.

N is for _____et.

Letter Recognition

84

Letter Nn

Nice Nate likes to share peanuts.

Draw a circle around each picture that begins with the sound of **Nn**. Then **color** all the pictures!

Letter Recognition

Letter

Can you find each **N** and **n** that is hidden in the room?

Color each **N purple** and each **n orange**. Then **color** the rest of the room!

Name _____

Letter **O** Uppercase

✏️ **Trace** the letters.

O ◯ ◯ ◯ ◯

◯ ◯ ◯ ◯ ◯

Letter **o** Lowercase

✏️ **Trace** the letters.

o ○ ○ ○ ○

○ ○ ○ ○ ○

These pictures begin with the letter **Oo**. 🖍️ **Color** the pictures.

Letter Recognition

Name _____

Letter

✏️ **Circle** the **O** or **o** in these words:

Olivia	owl	octopus	once
flower	cat	only	Owen
apple	yes	Omaha	out

✏️ **Circle** the pictures that start with the sound of **Oo**.
Color the pictures. 🖍

Name _____

These words start with **O** or **o**.

Write the lowercase **o** on the line.
Color the pictures.

O is for _____strich.

O is for _____ven.

O is for _____ctopus.

89

Letter Recognition

Letter Oo

See what has 8 legs and lives in the ocean.

Color the spaces with **Oo brown. Color** the other spaces **blue**.

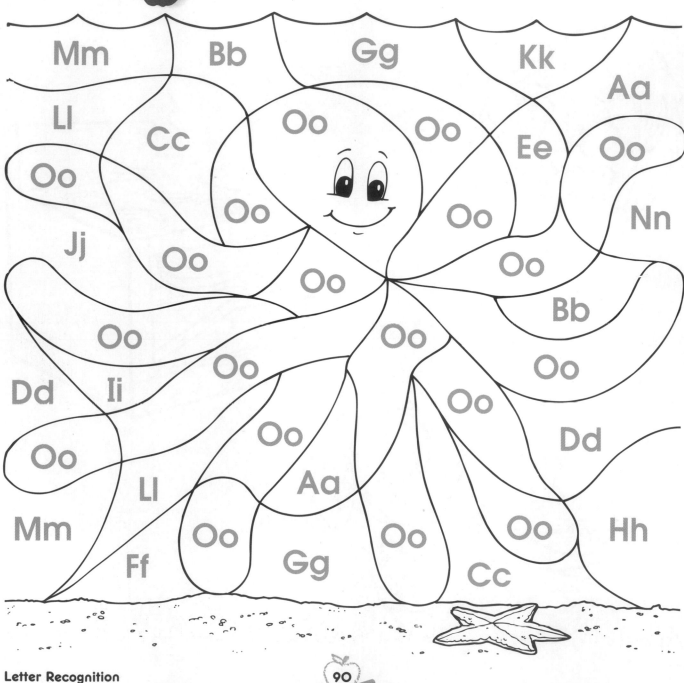

Mm Bb Gg Kk Aa Ll Cc Oo Oo Ee Oo Oo Oo Nn Jj Oo Oo Oo Bb Oo Oo Oo Oo Dd Ii Oo Dd Oo Ll Aa Oo Hh Mm Ff Oo Gg Oo Cc

Name _____

Letter

Color the **O**'s with the color named.

Trace and **color** the petals.
Color the picture.

orange

yellow

red

Letter Recognition

Name _____

Practice **writing** the letters **Aa-Oo** by **tracing** the **UPPER** and **lowercase** letters below.

Aa Bb Cc Dd Ee

Ff Gg Hh Ii Jj

Kk Ll Mm Nn Oo

Aa Bb Cc Dd Ee

Ff Gg Hh Ii Jj

Kk Ll Mm Nn Oo

✏️ **Trace** the letters **Aa-Oo**. Then practice **writing** them on the lines below.

Aa Bb Cc Dd Ee

Ff Gg Hh Ii Jj

Kk Ll Mm Nn Oo

93

Review A-O

Name _____

The Mouse on the Moon

Connect the dots from **A-O**. What do you see?

A
O
B
N
C
D
M
E
Mouse
L
J   K   F
I   H   G

Review A-O

Name _____

Climb the ladder and ✏️ **trace** the letters to save the princess!

Save the princess by climbing the alphabet ladder!

A B C D E F G H I J K L M N O

Review Letters A-O

Name _____

Connect the dots as you say the alphabet, starting with the letter **a**.

What do you see?

.n

.b

m.

.c

o. .a

.d

l.

i. .g

h

k.

.e

j

f

96

Review A-O

Name _____

Alphabet Camping

Trace the letters on the tent.
Color the picture!

97

Name _____

Letter P Uppercase

✏️ **Trace** the letters.

P   P   P   P   P

P   P   P   P   P

Letter P Lowercase

✏️ **Trace** the letters.

p   p   p   p   p

p   p   p   p   p

These pictures begin with the letter **Pp**. 🖍️ **Color** the pictures.

PENCIL

Name _____

Letter Pp

✏ **Circle** the **P** or **p** in these words:

pencil	Paul	balloon	pig
dog	party	penny	Patty
pumpkin	pie	pen	play

✏ **Circle** the pictures that start with the sound of **Pp**.
Color the pictures.

Letter Recognition

Name _____

These words start with **P** or **p**.

___ **Write** the **lowercase p** on the line.
Color the pictures.

P is for _____ig.

P is for _____in.

P is for _____an.

Letter Pp

If the picture begins with the sound of **Pp**, leave the space **white**.

Color all of the other spaces **red** to find a popping good snack!

Letter Recognition

Name _____

Letter

P p

Color each **P** or **p** on the pizza **red**. Then **color** the rest of the pizza.

Name _____

Letter Q Uppercase

Trace the letters.

Q Q Q Q Q

Q Q Q Q Q

Letter q Lowercase

Trace the letters.

q q q q q

q q q q q

These pictures begin with the letter **Qq**. **Color** the pictures.

LIBERTY
IN GOD
WE TRUST
2003

103

Name _____

Letter Qq

Circle the **Q** or **q** in these words:

pop	Quincy	quarter	quilt
bike	quit	Quinn	quiet
balloon	Mary	quail	fun

Circle the pictures that start with the sound of **Qq**.
Color the pictures.

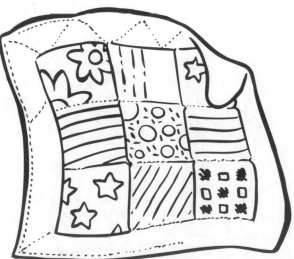

Letter Recognition

104

Name _____

These words start with **Q** or **q**.

Write the **lowercase q** on the line.
Color the pictures.

Q is for _____uilt.

Q is for _____ueen.

Q is for _____uarter.

105

Letter Qq

Name _____

Color the sections of pictures that begin with the sound of **Qq** red. **Color** all of the other sections yellow.

Name _____

Look how quiet everything in the picture seems.

Can you find each **Q** and **q**? **Color** each **Q blue** and each **q yellow**.

Letter Recognition

Name _____

Letter R Uppercase

✏️ **Trace** the letters.

R R R R R

R R R R R

Letter r Lowercase

✏️ **Trace** the letters.

r r r r r

r r r r r

These pictures begin with the letter **Rr**. 🖍️ **Color** the pictures.

Name _____

Letter

R r

Circle the **R** or **r** in these words:

rain   roses   Robert   nuts

rake   rabbit   pin   four

red   ring   Renee   rocket

Circle the pictures that start with the sound of **Rr**.
Color the pictures.

Letter Recognition

Name _____

These words start with **R** or **r**.

✏️ **Write** the **lowercase r** on the line.
Color the pictures. 🖍️

R is for _____abbit.

R is for _____attle.

R is for _____accoon.

Letter Recognition

110

Name _____

Letter Rr

Help Rodeo Raccoon rope the **R**'s.

Draw a circle around each picture that begins with the sound of **Rr. Color** the picture with fun colors for Rodeo Raccoon!

111

Letter Recognition

Name _____

Trace each **R** and **r**. **Color** each raindrop with **R green**. **Color** each raindrop with **r blue**. Use the same colors for the letters on the umbrella.

Letter **Rr**

Name _____

Letter S Uppercase — Trace the letters.

S   S   S   S   S

S   S   S   S   S

Letter s Lowercase — Trace the letters.

s   s   s   s   s

s   s   s   s   s

These pictures begin with the letter **Ss**. **Color** the pictures.

Letter Recognition

Name _____

Circle the **S** or **s** in these words:

sun	see	milk	six
Sam	saw	men	sailboat
Susie	sea	silly	swan

Circle the pictures that start with the sound of **Ss**.
Color the pictures.

Name _____

These words start with **S** or **s**.

 **Write** the **lowercase s** on the line.
Color the pictures.

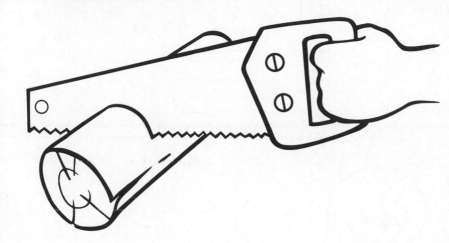

S is for _____aw.

S is for _____un.

S is for _____nake.

115

Letter Recognition

Name _____

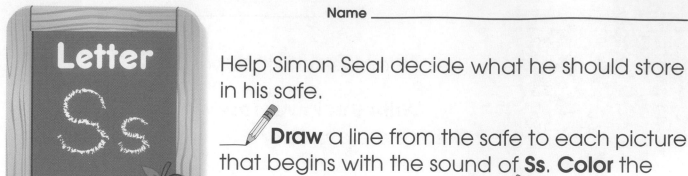

Letter Ss

Help Simon Seal decide what he should store in his safe.

Draw a line from the safe to each picture that begins with the sound of **Ss**. **Color** the pictures with bright colors!

Name _____

Letter Ss

Trace each **S** and **s**.

Color each bubble with **S** yellow. **Color** each bubble with **s** purple.

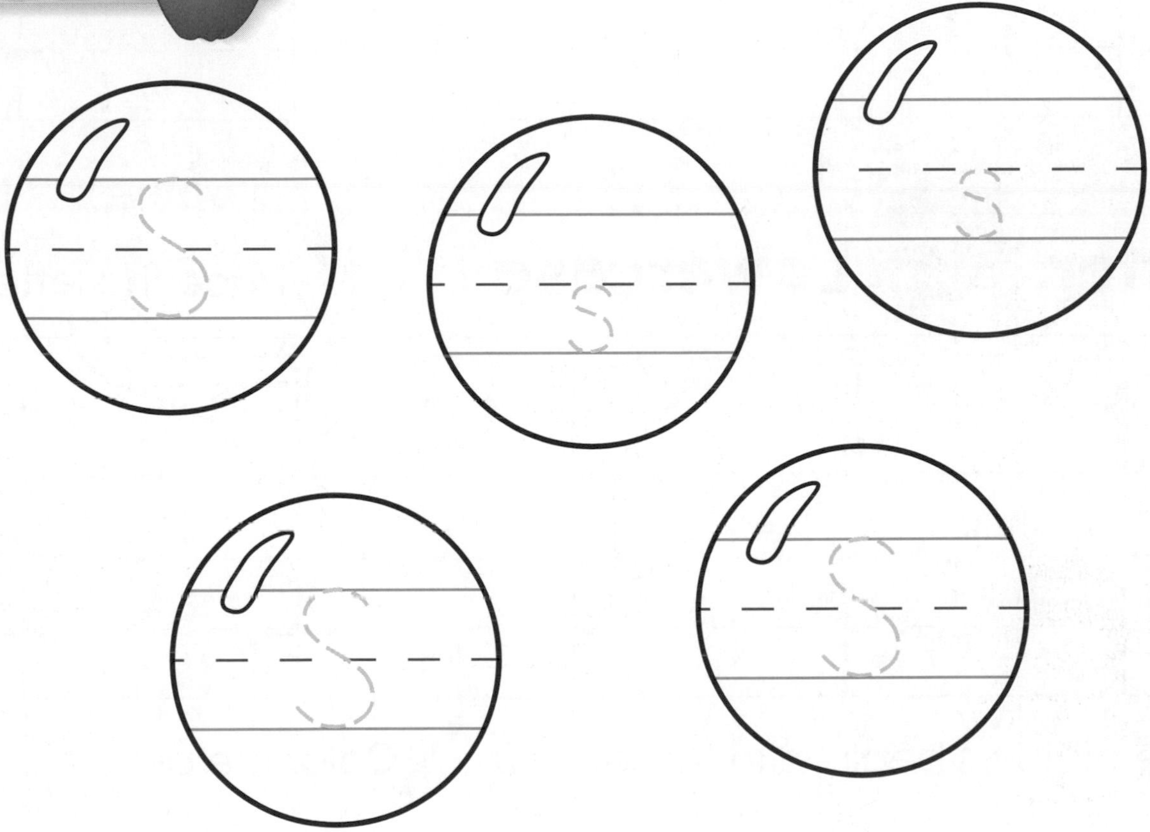

Soap

Letter **T** Uppercase

Trace the letters.

Letter **t** Lowercase

Trace the letters.

These pictures begin with the letter **Tt**. **Color** the pictures.

Name _____

Letter

Circle the **T** or **t** in these words:

Taylor   four   table   tiger

girl   Timothy   two   fish

television   telephone   time

Circle the pictures that start with the sound of **Tt**.
Color the pictures.

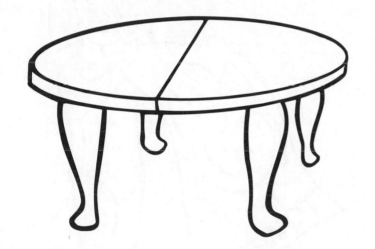

119

Letter Recognition

Name _____

These words start with **T** or **t**.

Write the **lowercase t** on the line.
Color the pictures.

T is for _____urtle.

T is for _____owel.

T is for _____ent.

TOWEL

Letter

Name _____

Color the pictures that begin with the sound of **Tt** orange. Then **color** the rest of the picture with bright colors.

Letter Recognition

Letter

Name _____

Do you like to play tic-tac-toe?

 **Color** each **T** and **t** with the correct color.
Draw a line to win tic-tac-toe.

T = red
t = green

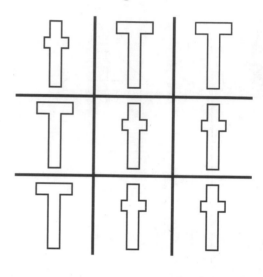

T = blue
t = yellow

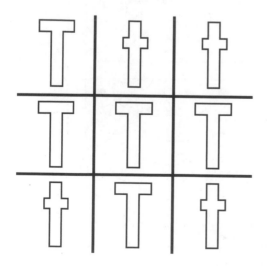

T = purple
t = orange

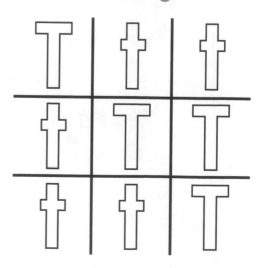

Review

Name _____

Trace the letters **Aa-Tt**. Then practice **writing** them on the lines below.

A a   B b   C c

D d   E e   F f

G g   H h   I i   J j

Name _____

Trace the letters **Aa-Tt**. Then practice **writing** them on the lines below.

Kk Ll Mm

Nn Oo Pp

Qq Rr Ss Tt

Review A-T

Name _____

What is the Rabbit Queen jumping out of?

_____ **Connect** the dots starting with the letter **A**, and you will see!

B · A ·

C ·

D · · E

F ·

G ·

H ·

I ·

J · · K · L

· T · S

· R

· Q

· P

· O

· N

· M

125

Review
A-T

Name _____

Who puts out fires and helps keep you safe?

Connect the dots as you say the alphabet, starting with the letter **a. Color** the picture.

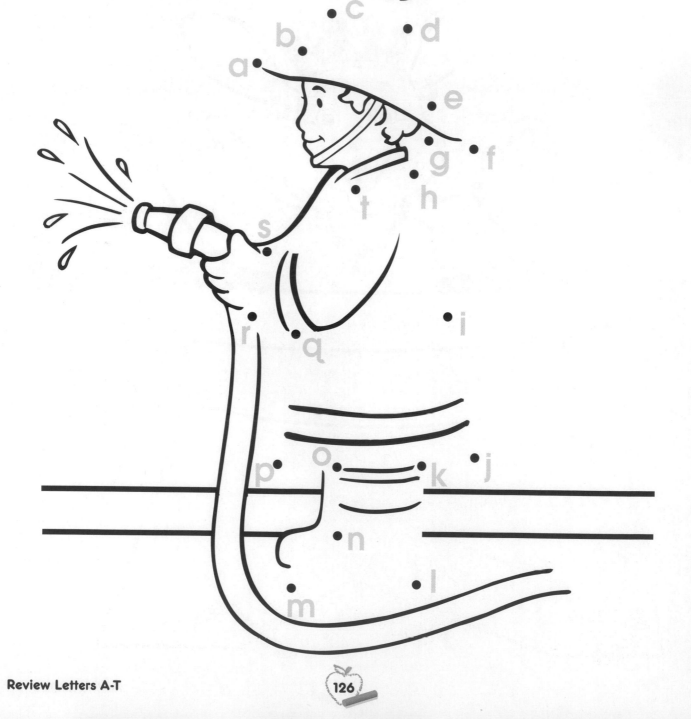

Review Letters A-T

126

Name _____

Review

Follow the maze and say each letter. Start with "**A**" for ant and end with "**T**" for turtle. **Color** the pictures!

B A C D E F G H I J K L M N O P Q R S T

LIBERTY
IN GOD WE TRUST
2003

127

Review Letters A-T

Name _____

Draw a line to connect the UPPER and lowercase letters that belong together. Color the pictures.

F

C

f

L

h

H

I

C

Review

A-T

Name _____

Draw a line to connect the **UPPER** and **lowercase** letters that belong together. **Color** the pictures.

 T

 S

 l

 R

 r

 S

 L

 t

129

Name _____

✏️ **Trace** the **UPPERCASE** letters **A-T**.

A	B	C	D
E	F	G	H
I	J	K	L
M	N	O	P
Q	R	S	T

Review Letters A-T

130

Name _____

✏ **Trace** the **lowercase** letters **a-t**. Then **write** the **UPPERCASE** letters from the page before with their matching **lowercase** letters on this page.

a	b	c	d
e	f	g	h
i	j	k	l
m	n	o	p
q	r	s	t

Review Letters A-T

Letter **U** Uppercase — Trace the letters.

U U U U U

U U U U U

Letter **U** Lowercase — Trace the letters.

u u u u u

u u u u u

These pictures begin with the letter **Uu**. **Color** the pictures.

U.S.A.

Hawaii

Alaska

Letter Uu

Name _____

✏️ **Circle** the **U** or **u** in these words:

under	unicorn	unless	for
umbrella	up	down	also
funny	flower	laugh	use

The letter **Uu** can have more than one sound. ✏️ **Circle** the pictures that start with the sound of **Uu**. 🖍️ **Color** the pictures.

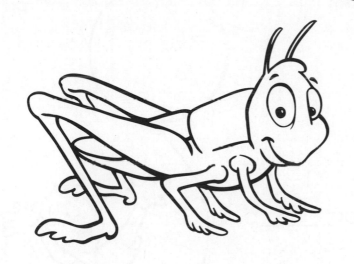

Letter Recognition

Name _____

These words start with **U** or **u**.

Write the **lowercase u** on the line.
Color the pictures.

U is for _____nicorn.

U is for _____p.

U is for _____mbrella.

Name _____

Letter Uu

Find each hidden **U** and **u**.

Color each **U** purple. **Color** each **u** orange. Then **color** the rest of the picture.

Letter Recognition

Name _____

Letter V Uppercase

Trace the letters.

V V V V V V

V V V V V

Letter v Lowercase

Trace the letters.

v v v v v v

v v v v v

These pictures begin with the letter **Vv**. **Color** the pictures.

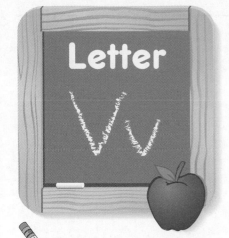

Letter
Vv

Name _____

Circle the **V** or **v** in these words:

Valerie	violin	rake	vest
Victor	valentine	look	van
rabbit	vacuum	vacation	up

Circle the pictures that start with the sound of **Vv**.
Color the pictures.

These words start with **V** or **v**.

Write the **lowercase v** on the line.
Color the pictures.

V is for _____est.

V is for _____ase.

V is for _____acuum.

Name _____

Letter

Vv

Help Vern Vampire vacuum.

Circle the pictures that begin with the sound of **Vv**. **Color** all the pictures.

139

Letter Recognition

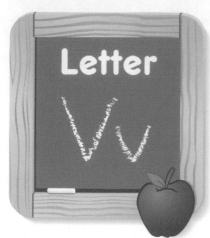

Letter Vv

Name _____

✏️ **Trace** each **V** and **v**.

🖍️ **Color** each heart with **V** or **v** red.

✏️ **Draw** a line from each **V** or **v** to one of the hearts on the left.

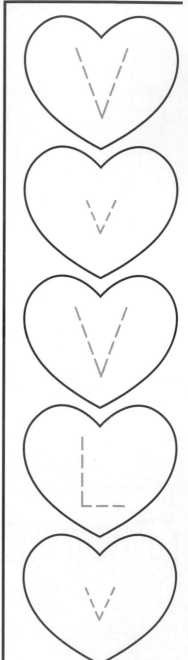

Letter W Uppercase

Trace the letters.

W W W W W W W W

W W W W W W

Letter W Lowercase

Trace the letters.

w w w w w w

w w w w w

These pictures begin with the letter **Ww**. **Color** the pictures.

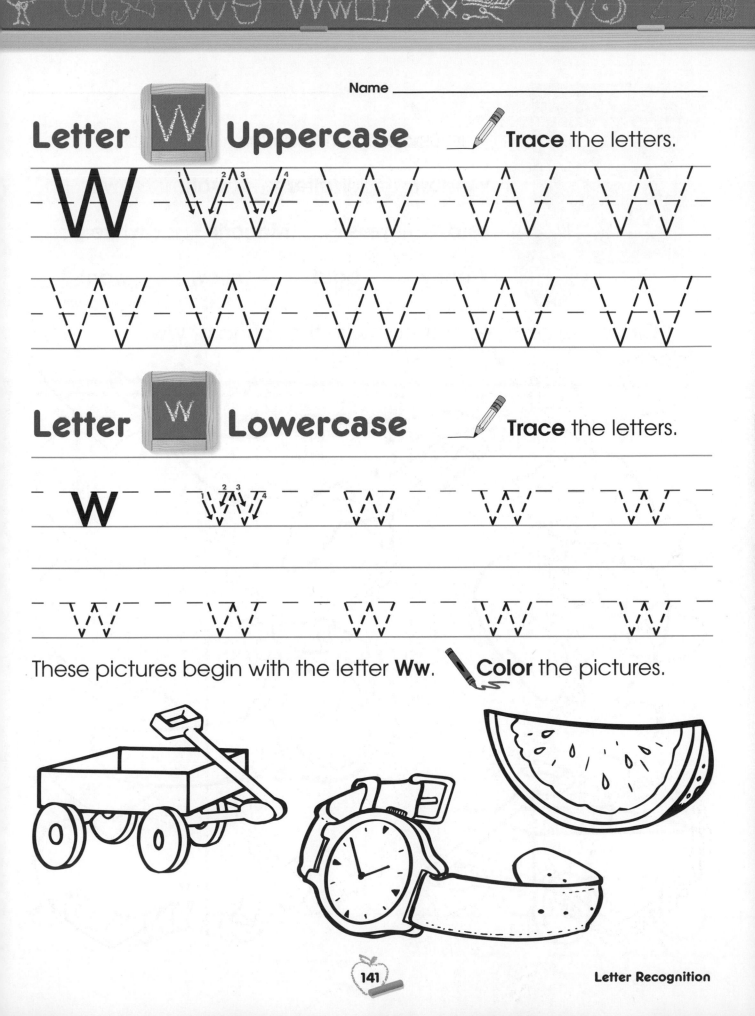

Letter Ww

Name _____

Circle the **W** or **w** in these words:

window	Walter	walk	win
said	was	Marjorie	white
Wendy	boat	willow	want

Circle the pictures that start with the sound of **Ww**.
Color the pictures.

Letter Recognition

Name _____

These words start with **W** or **w**.

Write the **lowercase w** on the line.
Color the pictures.

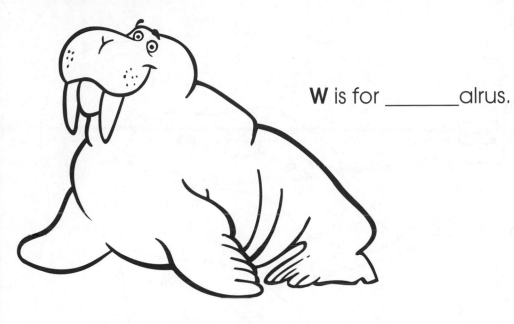

W is for _____alrus.

W is for _____atermelon.

W is for _____agon.

Letter Recognition

Name _____

Letter

Ww

Help the spider find its home.

Draw a line to follow each **W** and **w**.
Color the picture.

n   B   F

M

I

W

L   W

W   W

I   W

N   W

W

E   N

W

m   W

W

W

W   Home
Sweet
Home

w

W

W   W   W   W

Name _____

Letter Ww

Color each of the pictures that begin with the sound of **Ww**. Then **draw** a line from each colored picture to a watch face.

Letter Recognition

Name _____

Letter X Uppercase

Trace the letters.

X

Letter x Lowercase

Trace the letters.

x

These pictures begin with the letter **Xx**. **Color** the pictures.

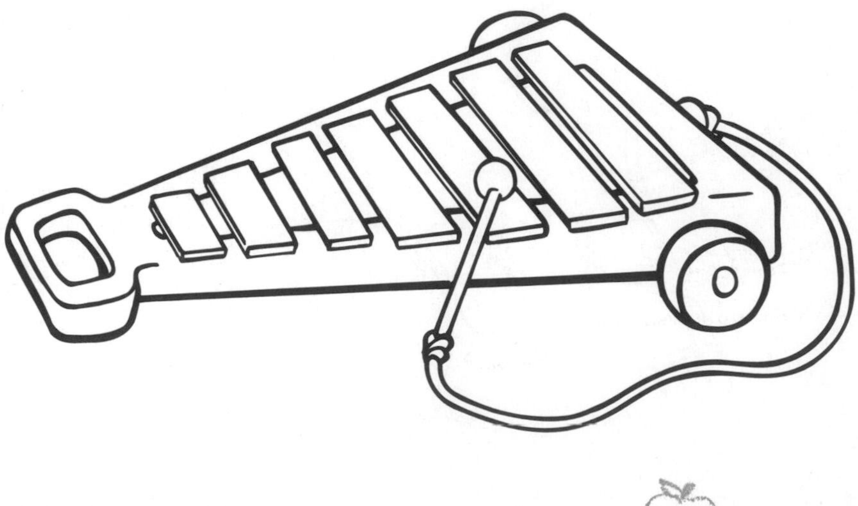

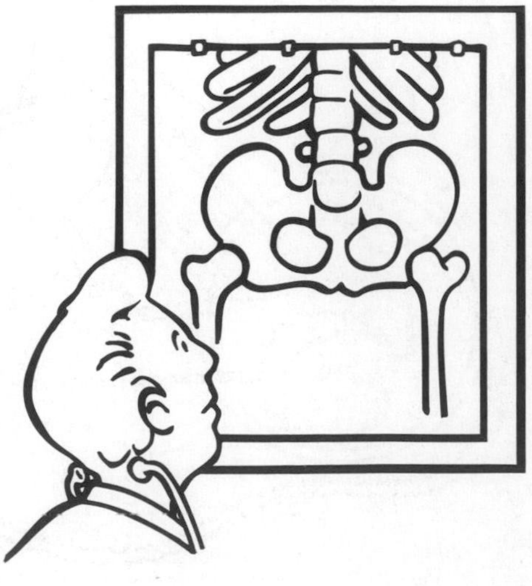

Name _____

Letter

Circle the **X** or **x** in these words:

Xavier	X ray	exit	dog
rabbit	Rex	xylophone	tax
excellent	exercise	play	bat

Circle the pictures that start with the sound of **Xx**.
Color the pictures.

EXIT

EXIT

147

Letter Recognition

Name _____

These words start with **X** or **x**.

Write the **lowercase x** on the line.
Color the pictures.

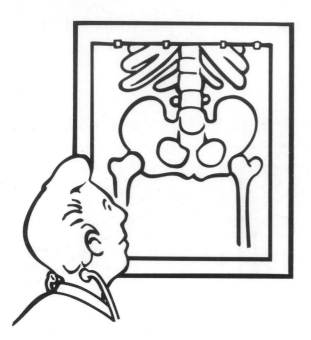

X is for _____ ray.

X is in E_____it.

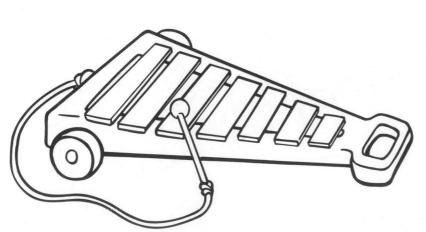

X is for _____ylophone.

Color the **UPPERCASE X**'s **red**. **Color** the lowercase **x**'s **blue**.

For each **UPPERCASE** letter, write its matching **lowercase** letter next to it. For each **lowercase** letter, write its matching **UPPERCASE** letter next to it.

149

Name _____

Letter Y Uppercase

✏️ **Trace** the letters.

Y - - Y - - Y - - Y - - Y

Y - - Y - - Y - - Y - - Y

Letter y Lowercase

✏️ **Trace** the letters.

y y y y y

y y y y y

These pictures begin with the letter **Yy**. 🖍️ **Color** the pictures.

Name _____

Circle the **Y** or **y** in these words:

yarn	yo-yo	yard	Yuri
Yvonne	yes	yoke	watch
vine	yesterday	yellow	us

Circle the pictures that start with the sound of **Yy**.
Color the pictures.

JAR

Letter Recognition

Name _____

These words start with **Y** or **y**.

Write the **lowercase y** on the line.
Color the pictures.

Y is for _____o-yo.

Y is for _____arn.

Yogurt

Y is for _____ogurt.

Name _____

Letter

Yy

Find each **Y** and **y** hidden in the yard.

Color each **Y red** and each **y** yellow.
Color the rest of the yard and make it fun!

Letter Recognition

Name _____

Letter Yy

Make this yo-yo spin.

Color only the pictures that begin with the sound of **Yy**.

Letter Z Uppercase

✏ **Trace** the letters.

Z

Z   Z   Z   Z   Z

Z   Z   Z   Z

Letter Z Lowercase

✏ **Trace** the letters.

z

z   z   z   z   z

z   z   z   z   z

These pictures begin with the letter **Zz**. 🖍 **Color** the pictures.

Letter Recognition

Name _____

Letter Zz

Circle the **Z** or **z** in these words:

zipper	zebra	last	zig-zag
jazz	Zelda	zoom	zero
frog	zone	lizard	zoo

Circle the pictures that start with the sound of **Zz**.
Color the pictures.

ZOOM!

Name _____

These words start with **Z** or **z**.

_____ **Write** the **lowercase z** on the line.
Color the pictures.

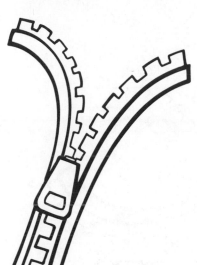

Z is for _____ipper.

Z is for _____ig-zag.

Z is for _____ebra.

Letter Recognition

Letter Zz

Name _____

Take a trip through the zoo.

Color only the pictures that begin with the sound of **Zz**.

Review A-Z

Name _____

Trace the letters **Aa-Zz**. Then practice **writing** them on the lines below.

Aa Bb Cc Dd

Ee Ff Gg Hh Ii

Jj Kk Ll Mm

159

Review Letters A-Z

Review A-Z

Name _____

✏️ **Trace** the letters **Aa-Zz**. Then practice **writing** them on the lines below.

Nn Oo Pp Qq

Rr Ss Tt Uu Vv

Ww Xx Yy Zz

Review Letters A-Z

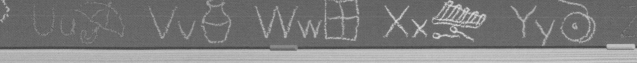

Name _____

Alphabet X ray

Trace all the letters in the X ray.
Color the picture.

Review Letters A-Z

Review A-Z

Name _____

Draw a line from **A-Z** to show the way to Grandma and Grandpa's house.

Review A-Z

Name _____

Draw a line from **A-Z** to show the way to P. Penguin's house.

Review Letters A-Z

Name _____

Review
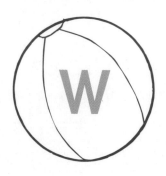

Draw a line between the **UPPER** and **lowercase** letters that belong together.

Review Letters A-Z

164

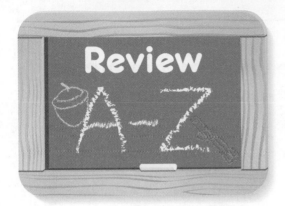

Review A-Z

Name _____

Draw a line between the **UPPER** and **lowercase** letters that belong together.

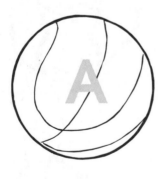

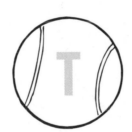

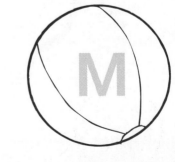

165

Review Letters A-Z

Review
A-Z

Name _____

Trace the UPPER and lowercase letters on each object. Color the pictures.

Review
A-Z

Name _____

Trace the **UPPER** and **lowercase** letters on each object. **Color** the pictures.

167

Review Letters A-Z

Review A-Z

Name _____

Trace the UPPER and lowercase letters on each object. Color the pictures.

RUFF

Kk

Dd

Nn

Rr

Pp

Review
A-Z

Name _____

Trace the UPPER and lowercase letters on each object. Color the pictures.

MILK MILK

Jj

Qq

Mm

Ll

Oo

Review Letters A-Z

Name _____

Review A-Z

Trace the **UPPER** and **lowercase** letters on each object. **Color** the pictures.

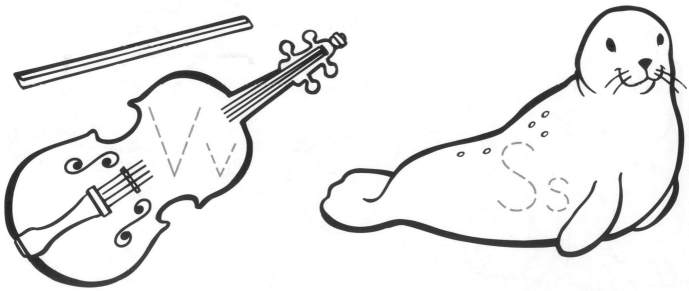

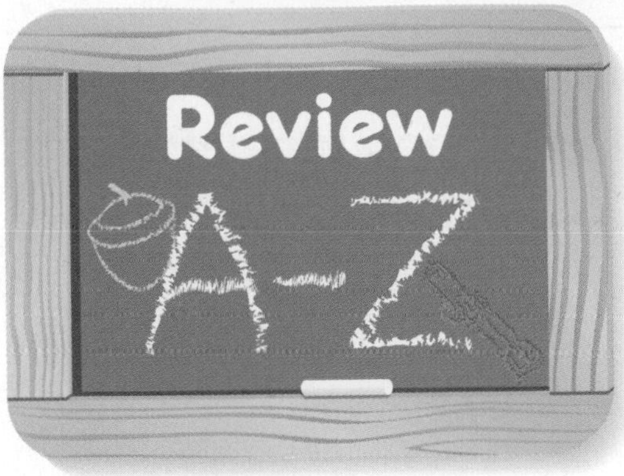

Review A-Z

Name _____

Trace the **UPPER** and **lowercase** letters on each object. **Color** the pictures.

Uu

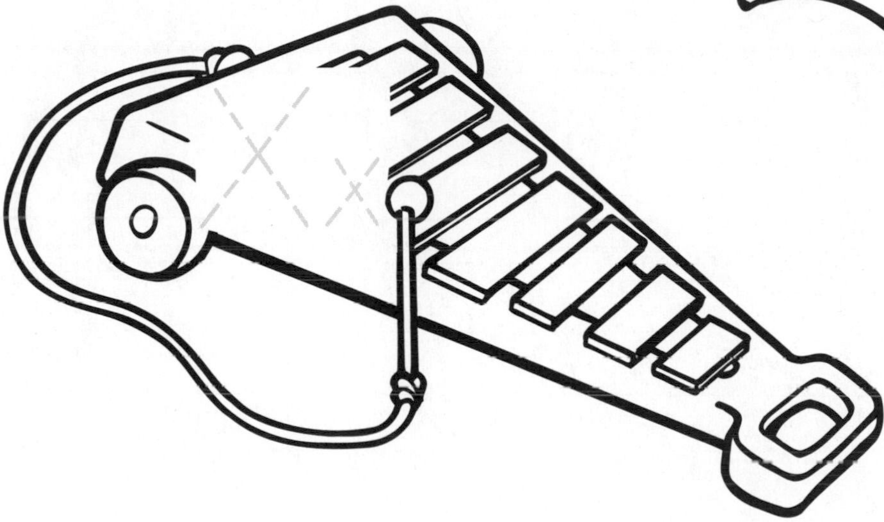

Xx

Yy

Ww

171

Review A-Z

Name _____

Draw a line between the **UPPER** and **lowercase** letters that belong together.

A

B

C

D

E

F

G

d

c

a

b

e

g

f

Review Letters A-Z

172

Review A-Z

✏️ **Draw** a line between the **UPPER** and **lowercase** letters that belong together.

H

I

J

K

L

M

i

h

l

j

m

k

Name _____

✏️ **Draw** a line between the **UPPER** and **lowercase** letters that belong together.

N

O

P

Q

R

S

T

p

o

n

r

q

t

s

Review Letters A-Z

Review A-Z

Name _____

✏️ **Draw** a line between the **UPPER** and **lowercase** letters that belong together.

U

V

W

X

Y

Z

V

W

u

z

x

y

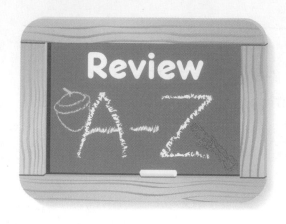

Review
A-Z

Connect the dots from **A-Z**. Use the correct color for each part of the line. What do you see?

A-F = red   F-I = yellow   I-N = blue
N-T = green   T-Z = purple

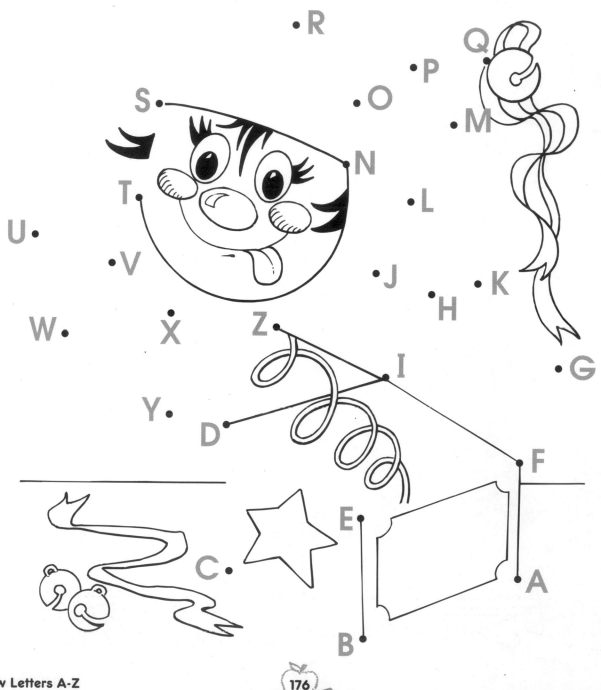

Review
A-Z

Name _____

Connect the dots as you say the alphabet, starting with the letter **A**. **Color** the picture.

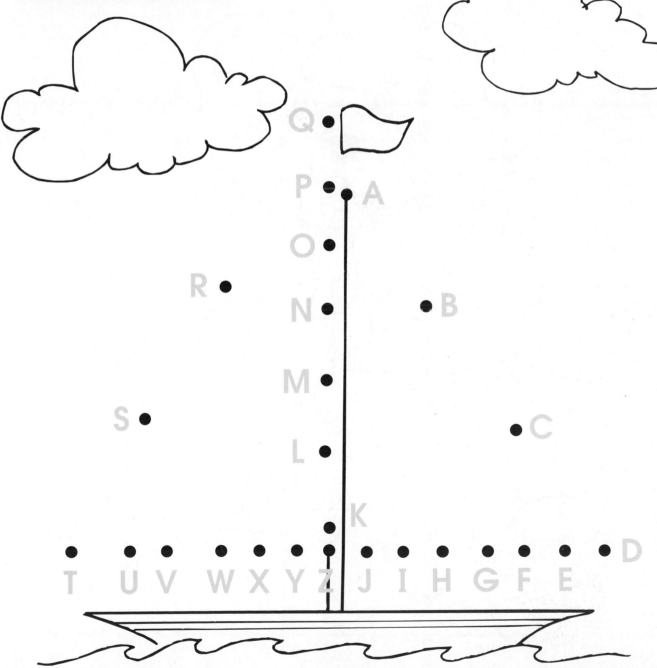

Review Letters A-Z

Review A-Z

Name _____

🖍 **Connect** the dots as you say the alphabet, starting with the letter **A**. **Color** the picture.

Review Letters A-Z

178

Review A-Z

Name _____

Connect the dots from **A-Z. Color** the gum balls with your favorite colors!

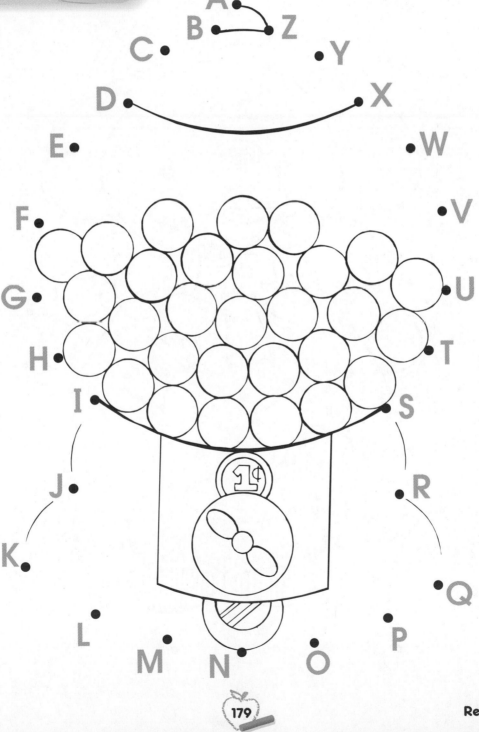

Review Letters A-Z

Review
A-Z

Connect the dots from **A-Z**.
Color the picture.

A B C D E F G H I J K L M N O P Q R S T U V W X Y Z

Review Letters A-Z

180

Review A-Z

Name _____

Connect the dots as you say the alphabet, starting with the letter **a**. **Color** the picture.

Stop

Review Letters A-Z

Review A-Z

Name _____

Connect the dots from **a-z**.
Color the picture.

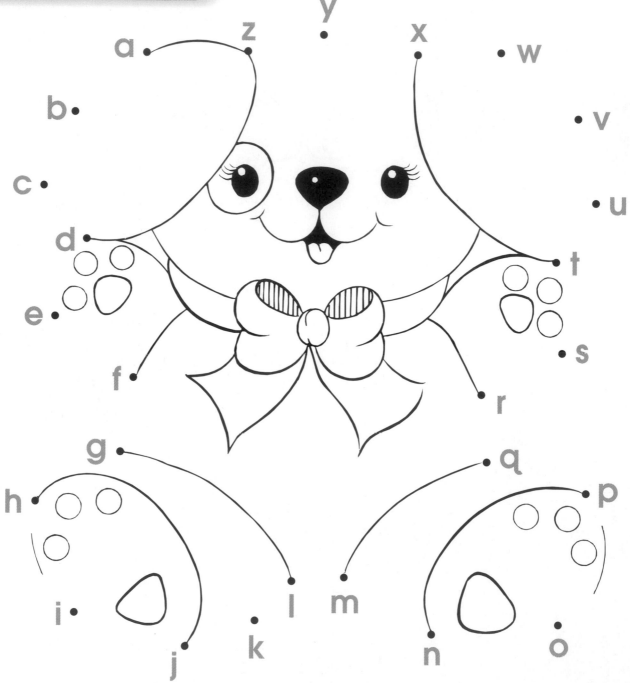

Review Letters A-Z

182

Name _____

Vowel Aa

Short Aa is the sound you hear at the beginning of the word **alligator**.

Color the pictures that begin with the sound of **short Aa**.

LUNCH

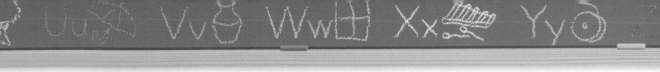

Beginning Consonant Bb

Name _____

Say each picture name. If the picture name begins with the same sound as **ball, color** the space with that picture.

Letter Sounds A-Z

Beginning Consonant
Cc

Give the caterpillar some spots.

Say the name of each picture. If the picture name begins with the same sound as **caterpillar**, **circle** the picture to make a spot.

Beginning Sounds

Aa Bb Cc

Name _____

Say the sound the letters make.

Circle the pictures in each row that begin with the sound of the letter shown.

Aa			
Aa			
Bb			
Bb			
Cc			
Cc			

Letter Sounds A-Z

Beginning Consonant
Dd

Name _____

Say the picture names in each box on the door.

Circle the picture whose name begins with the same sound as **dinosaur**.

Vowel **Ee**

Name _____

Short Ee is the sound you hear at the beginning of the word **eggs**.

Color the eggs with pictures that begin with the sound of **short Ee**.

Beginning Consonant Ff

Look at the bubbles below. Say each picture name. If the picture name begins with the same sound as **fish**, **color** the bubble **blue**.

Beginning Sounds

Dd Ee Ff

Name _____

Say the sound the letters make.

Circle the pictures in each row that begin with the sound of the letter shown.

Dd			
Dd			
Ee			
Ee			
Ff			
Ff			

Letter Sounds A-Z

Beginning Consonant Gg

Name _____

Say each picture name.

✏ **Circle** the pictures whose names begin with the same sound as **goggles**.

Beginning Consonant

Hh

Say each picture name. If the picture name begins with the sound of **Hh**, **color** the hat.

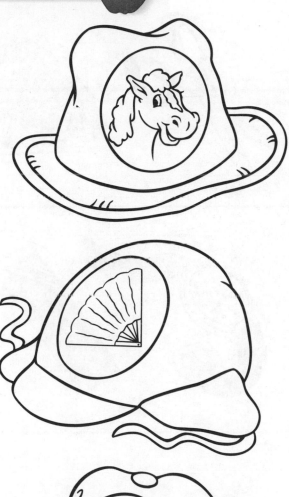

Beginning Sounds

Ff Gg Hh

Name _____

Say the sound the letters make.

Circle the pictures in each row that begin with the sound of the letter shown.

Ff	  
Gg	 
Hh	  

Name _____

Vowel

Short Ii is the sound you hear at the beginning of the word **igloo**.

Color the pictures that begin with the sound of **short Ii**.

195

Name _____

Beginning Sounds
Gg Hh Ii

Say the sound the letters make.

Circle the pictures in each row that begin with the sound of the letter shown.

Gg			
Gg			
Hh			
Hh			
Ii			
Ii			

Beginning Consonant

What is Jamie wearing today?

Say each picture name.

Color the spaces whose picture names begin with the sound of **Jj blue**. **Color** the other spaces yellow.

◆ What is Jamie wearing? _____

Beginning Consonant

Kk

Name _____

Look at the pictures on the kite's tail. Say each picture name. If the picture name begins with the same sound as **kite**, **color** that part of the tail **orange**. Then **color** the kite.

Letter Sounds A-Z

198

Name _____

Beginning Consonant
Ll

What belongs in the lion's cage?

Color only those pictures whose names begin with the same sound as **ladder**.

199

Letter Sounds A-Z

Name _____

Beginning Sounds

Jj Kk Ll

Say the sound the letters make.

Circle the pictures in each row that begin with the sound of the letter shown.

Jj			
Jj			
Kk			
Kk			
Ll			
Ll			

200

Name _____

Beginning Consonant Mm

Say each picture name.

Color the pictures whose names begin with the same sound as **macaroni** and **meatballs**.

Letter Sounds A-Z

Beginning Consonant

Nn

Help the baby birds find their nest.

✏️ **Draw** a line to follow the path with the pictures whose names begin with the same sound as **nest**.

Name _____

Vowel

Short Oo is the sound you hear at the beginning of the word **otter**.

Color the pictures that begin with the sound of **short Oo**.

203

Letter Sounds A-Z

Name _____

Beginning Sounds

Mm Nn Oo

Say the sound the letters make.

Circle the pictures in each row that begin with the sound of the letter shown.

Mm			
Mm			
Nn			
Nn			
Oo			
Oo			

Beginning Consonant

Name _____

Pam packs only things whose names begin with the same sound as **panda**. Say the picture names.

Circle each picture whose name begins with the same sound as **Pam** and **panda**.

Letter Sounds A-Z

Beginning Sounds

Name _____

Say the sound the letters make.

Circle the pictures in each row that begin with the sound of the letter shown.

Mm	  
Nn	  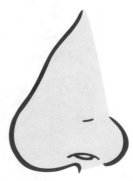
Pp	  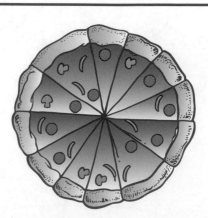

Name _____

Beginning Consonant Qq

Look at the pictures on the quilt below. Say each picture name. If the picture name begins with the same sound as **quilt**, **color** the square yellow. **Color** the other squares **purple**.

Letter Sounds A-Z

Beginning Consonant

Rr

Name _____

Who is the raccoon going to visit?

Say each picture name.

Color the spaces with pictures whose names begin with the same sound as **raccoon**.

Who is the raccoon going to visit?_____

Beginning Sounds
Pp Qq Rr

Name _____

Say the sound the letters make.

Circle the pictures in each row that begin with the sound of the letter shown.

Pp			
Pp			
Qq			
Qq			
Rr			
Rr			

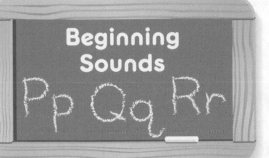

Letter Sounds A-Z

Beginning Consonant
Ss

Name _____

Find the letter **S**.

Say each picture name. If the picture name begins with the same sound as **six**, **color** the space **blue**. **Color** the other spaces **orange**. Do you see the **S**?

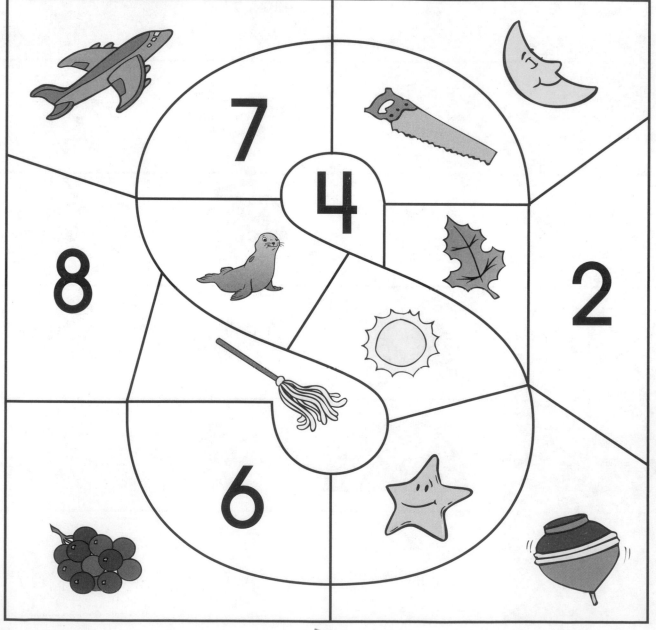

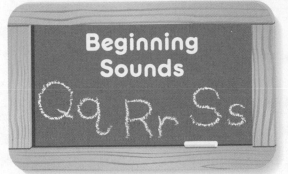

Beginning Sounds

Qq Rr Ss

Name _____

Say each picture name. Say the letters.

Draw a line from each picture to its matching letter.

Qq

Rr

Ss

211

Letter Sounds A-Z

Beginning Consonant
T t

Name _____

Say the picture name for each toy in the tub.

Draw an **X** on the pictures whose names begin with the same sound as **tub**.

Name _____

Vowel

Uu

Only the pictures whose names begin with the sound of **short Uu** belong under the umbrella. **Color** these pictures.

213

Name _____

Beginning Sounds
Ss Tt Uu

Say the sound the letters make.

Circle the pictures in each row that begin with the sound of the letter shown.

Ss			
Ss			
Tt			
Tt			
Uu			
Uu			

Letter Sounds A-Z

Name _____

Beginning Consonant

Vv

The vacuum cleaner picks up only pictures whose names begin with the sound of **Vv**. **Color** these pictures.

BE
MINE

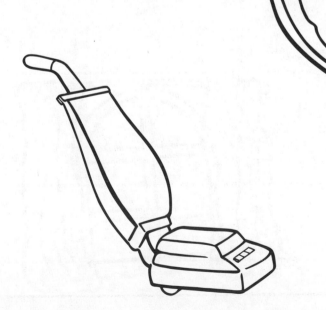

215

Name _____

Beginning Consonant Ww

The wagon can carry only pictures whose names begin with the sound of **Ww**. **Color** these pictures.

Beginning Sounds
Tt Vv Ww

Say the sound the letters make.

Circle the pictures in each row that begin with the sound of the letter shown.

Tt	  
Vv	  
Ww	  

Letter Sounds A-Z

Consonant

X X

Color the pictures that have the sound of **Xx** in them.

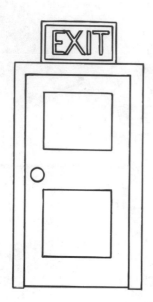

EXIT

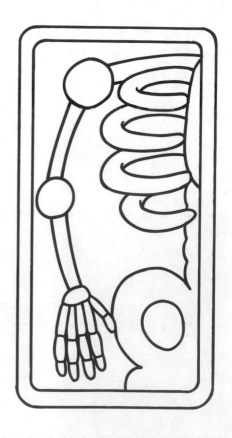

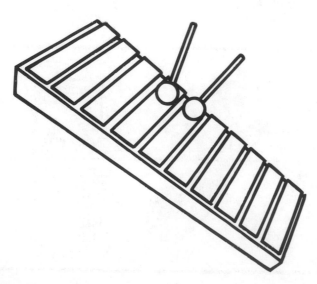

Letter Sounds A-Z

218

Beginning Sounds

Vv Ww Xx

Name _____

Say the sound the letters make.

Circle the pictures in each row that begin with the sound of the letter shown.

Vv			
Vv			
Ww			
Ww			
Xx			
Xx			

Letter Sounds A-Z

Beginning Consonant

Yy

Name _____

Say each picture name.

Draw a **green** line from each ball of yarn to the pictures whose names begin with the sound of **Yy**.

Name _____

Beginning Consonant Zz

Say each picture name.

Color the pictures whose names begin with the sound of **Zz**.

Letter Sounds A-Z

Name _____

Say the sound the letters make.

Circle the pictures in each row that begin with the sound of the letter shown.

Xx			
Yy			
Zz	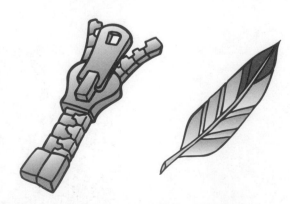		

Name _____

Beginning Sounds
Yy Zz

Say the sound the letters make.

Circle the pictures in each row that begin with the sound of the letter shown.

Yy			
Yy			Yogurt
Zz			
Zz			0

Letter Sounds A-Z

Review A-Z

Name _____

Say the name of each picture.

✏️ **Write** the letter that makes the beginning sound for each picture.

_ _ _ _ ar

_ _ _ _ ipper

_ _ _ _ ite

_ _ _ _ etter

_ _ _ _ oat

_ _ _ _ ose

_ _ _ _ un

_ _ _ _ ouse

_ _ _ _ urtle

_ _ _ _ lasses

_ _ _ _ ar

_ _ _ _ og

Name _____

Ending Consonant Sounds

Look at the picture in each box.

Color the pictures in that row that end with the same sound.

  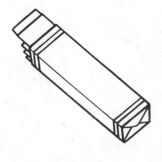 

Letter Sounds A-Z

Ending Consonant Sounds

Name _____

Look at the picture in each box.

✏️ **Circle** the pictures in that row that have the same ending sound.

Name _____

Ending Consonant Sounds

Say the name of each picture.

✏️ **Write** the letter to complete each word.

ha

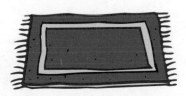

ru

da

ja

pi

re

Letter Sounds A-Z

Beginning and Ending Consonants

Name _____

Say the name of each picture.

Draw a **blue** circle around the picture if it begins with the sound of the letter below it. **Draw** a **green** triangle around the picture if it ends with the sound of the letter below it.

w

l

m

k

n

v

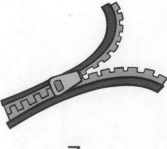

t

s

z

Beginning and Ending Consonants

Say the name of each picture.

Draw a triangle around the letter that makes the beginning sound. **Draw** a square around the letter that makes the ending sound. **Color** the pictures.

o   r   t

f   d   w

v   t   b

x   c   r

t   g   d

d   a   k

l   t   h

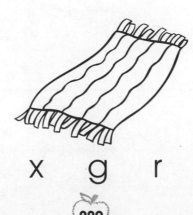

x   g   r

p   t   v

Short Vowels

Vowels are the letters **a**, **e**, **i**, **o**, and **u**. Short **a** is the sound you hear in **ant**. Short **e** is the sound you hear in **elephant**. Short **i** is the sound you hear in **igloo**. Short **o** is the sound you hear in **octopus**. Short **u** is the sound you hear in **umbrella**.

Say the short vowel sound at the beginning of each row. Say the name of each picture. Then **color** the pictures in each row that have the same short vowel sounds as that letter.

ă				
ĕ				
ĭ				
ŏ				
ŭ				

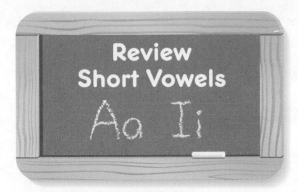

Review Short Vowels
Aa Ii

Name _____

Say each picture name.

Circle the vowel sound you hear.

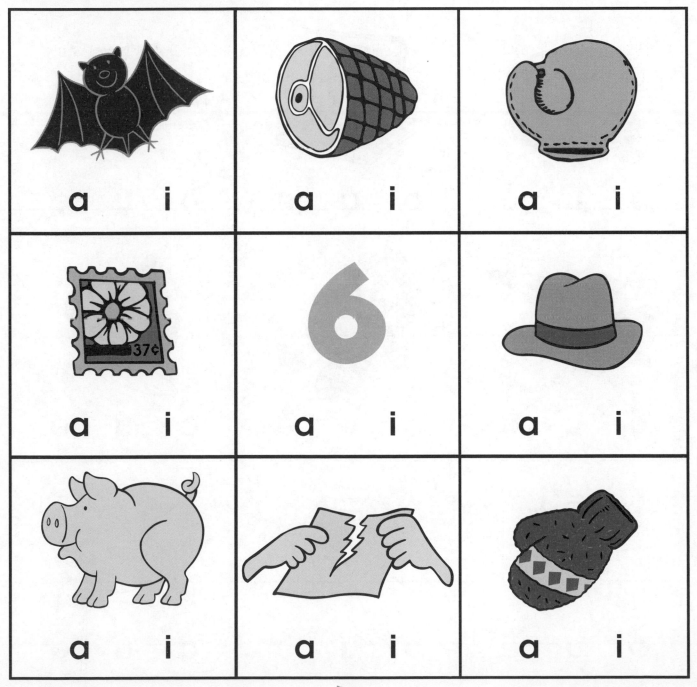

a i	a i	a i
a i	a i	a i
a i	a i	a i

231

Name _____

Review
Short Vowels
Oo Uu Ee

Say each picture name.

Circle the vowel sound you hear.

o u e	o u e	o u e
o u e	o u e	o u e
o u e	o u e	o u e

Name _____

Look at each picture.

 Draw a line to the letter that makes the same vowel sound.

a

e

i

o

u

Letter Sounds A-Z

Long Vowels

Vowels are the letters **a, e, i, o,** and **u.** Long vowel sounds say their own names. Long **a** is the sound you hear in **hay.** Long **e** is the sound you hear in **me.** Long **i** is the sound you hear in **pie.** Long **o** is the sound you hear in **no.** Long **u** is the sound you hear in **cute.**

Say the long vowel sound at the beginning of each row. Say the name of each picture. Then **color** the pictures in each row that have the same long vowel sounds as that letter.

ā		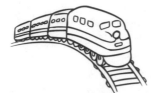		
ē				
ī				
ō				
ū				

Name _____

**Circle** the word if it has a long vowel sound.
Remember, a long vowel says its name.

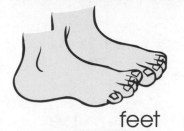

feet

snake

cup

hose

tie

hat

dog

rake

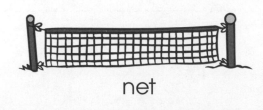

bug

bone

bib

net

Letter Sounds A-Z

Name _____

Short and Long Vowels

Say the name of each picture.

✏️ **Write** the vowel on each line that completes the word. 🖍️ **Color** the short vowel pictures. ✏️ **Circle** the long vowel pictures.

a   e   i   o   u

 j___g

 l___af

 l___ck

 c___be

 k___te

 t___pe

 p___n

 c___t

 b___ll

r___pe

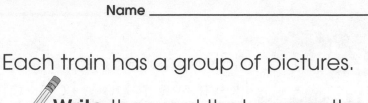

Name _____

Words With a

Each train has a group of pictures.

✏️ **Write** the word that names the pictures. Read your rhyming words.

These trains use the short **a** sound as in the word **cat**.

These trains use the long **a** sound as in the word **lake**.

237

Letter Sounds A-Z

Words With e

Short **e** sounds like the **e** in **hen**. Long **e** sounds like the **e** in **bee**. Look at the pictures. If the word has a short **e** sound, **draw** a line to the **hen** with your **red** crayon. If the word has a long **e** sound, **draw** a line to the **bee** with your **green** crayon.

hen

bee

Name _____

Words With

Short **i** sounds like the **i** in **pig**. Long **i** sounds like the **i** in **kite**.

Draw a circle around the words with the short **i** sound. **Draw** an **X** on the words with the long **i** sound.

five

pig

pin

slide

kite

lid

tie

bib

pie

Letter Sounds A-Z

Name _____

Words With O

The short **o** sounds like the **o** in **dog**. Long **o** sounds like the **o** in **rope**.

✏️ **Draw** a line from the picture to the word that names it. ✏️ **Draw** a circle around the word if it has a short **o** sound.

hot dog

fox

blocks

rose

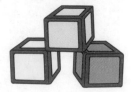

boat

Words With u

The short **u** sounds like the **u** in **bug**. Long **u** sounds like the **u** in **blue**.

Draw a circle around the words with the short **u** sound. **Draw** an **X** on the words with the long **u** sound.

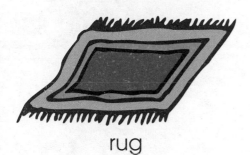

rug

cup

music

tub

suit

glue

bug

puppy

gum

241

Review

Name _____

✏️ **Write** the vowel on each line that completes the word.

a e i o u

c____t

b____k____

sm____k____

tr_____

c____b

p____n

m____m

b____b

d____d

d____ck

Name _____

✏ Keep this list handy and add more words to it.

short a
(ă as in **cat**)

_____ _ _ _ _ _ _ _

_____

short e
(ĕ as in **get**)

_____ _ _ _ _ _ _ _

_____

short i
(ĭ as in **pin**)

_____ _ _ _ _ _ _ _

_____

short o
(ŏ as in **cot**)

_____ _ _ _ _ _ _ _

_____

short u
(ŭ as in **cut**)

_____

_____

long a
(ā as in **train**)

_____ _ _ _ _ _ _ _

_____

long e
(ē as in **tree**)

_____ _ _ _ _ _ _ _

_____

long i
(ī as in **ice**)

_____ _ _ _ _ _ _ _

_____

long o
(ō as in **boat**)

_____ _ _ _ _ _ _ _

_____

long u
(ū as in **cube**)

_____

_____

Letter Sounds A-Z

Name _____

Super Silent

When you add an **e** to the end of some words, the vowel changes from a short vowel sound to a long vowel sound. **Example:** rip + **e** = ripe.

Say the word under the first picture in each pair. Then add an **e** to the word under the next picture. Say the new word.

pet _____

tub _____

man _____

kit _____

pin _____

cap _____

Name _____

Consonant Blends

bl fl sl

Consonant blends are two or more consonant sounds together in a word. The blend is made by combining the consonant sounds.
Example: floor

The name of each picture begins with a **blend**.
Circle the beginning blend for each picture.

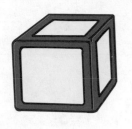

bl fl cl

cl fl gl

fl bl pl

fl cl gl

pl gl cl

gl fl sl

gl fl cl

sl fl cl

cl gl sl

Letter Sounds A-Z

Consonant Blends

sp st
sw

Draw a line from the picture to the blend that begins its word.

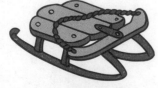

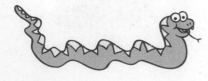

sk

sl

sm

sn

sp

st

sw

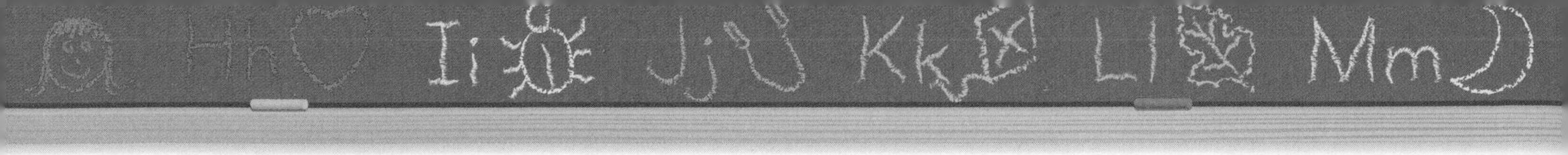

Name _____

Ending Consonant Blends

ft lt

✏ **Write lt** or **ft** to complete the words.

be _____

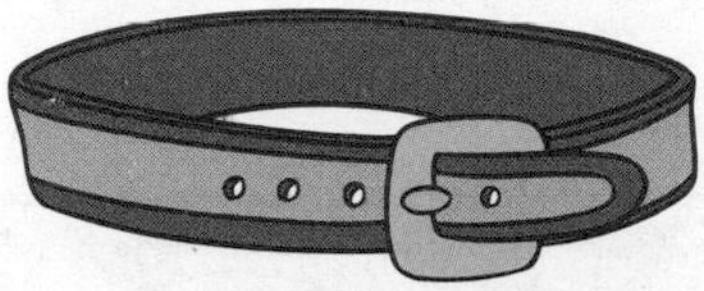

ra _____

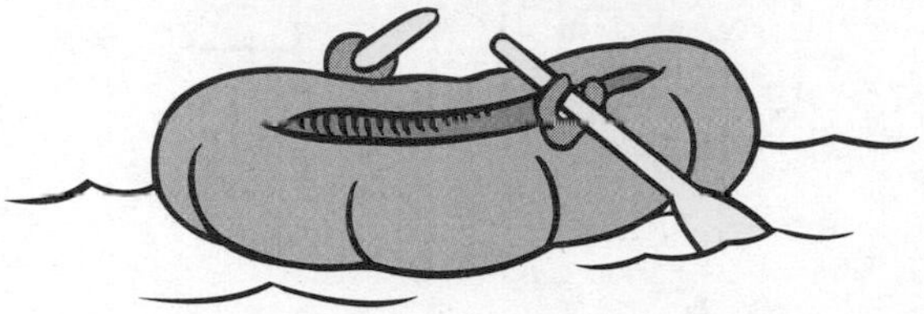

sa _____

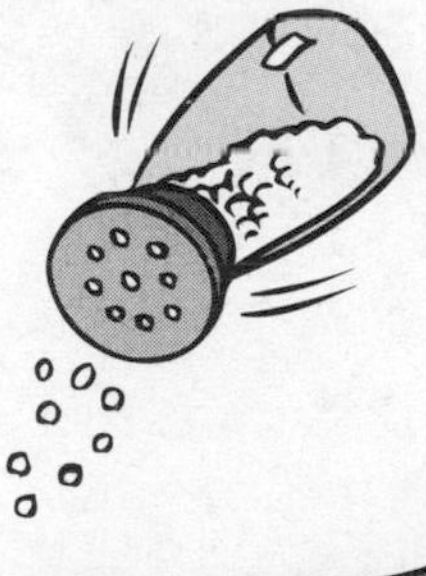

qui _____

le _____

Ending Consonant Blends

lf st lk
sk lk

Name _____

Draw a line from the picture to the blend that ends the word.

lf

lk

sk

st

Letter Sounds A-Z

248

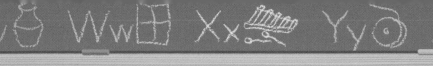

Name _____

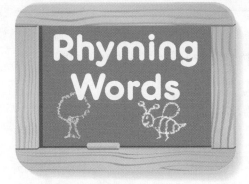

Rhyming words are words that sound alike at the end of the word. **Fish** and **dish** rhyme.

Circle the picture in each row that rhymes with the first picture.

Letter Sounds A-Z

Rhyming Words

Name _____

Draw a line to match each rhyming picture. **Color** the pictures.

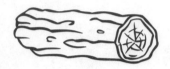

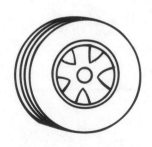

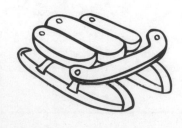

Name _____

Rhyming Words

Say each word pair aloud.

Draw a circle around each word pair that rhymes. **Draw** an **X** on each pair that does not rhyme.

Example:

(soap rope)	red dog	book hook
cold rock	cat hat	yellow black
one two	rock sock	rat flat
good nice	you to	meet toy
old sold	sale whale	word letter

Letter Sounds A-Z

Name _____

Draw a line to match the pictures that rhyme. **Write** two of your rhyming word pairs below.

_____   _____

- - - - - - - - - -   - - - - - - - - - -

_____   _____

- - - - - - - - - -   - - - - - - - - - -

_____   _____

Name _____

Practice by **tracing** the letter. Then **write** the letter.

A A A A A A A

a a a a a a

Name _____

✏️ Practice by **tracing** the words. Then **write** the words.

alligator

apple

ant

Alaska

Printing Letters and Words

Name _____

Practice by **tracing** the letter. Then **write** the letter.

B B B B B B B

b b b b b b

Name _____

Practice by **tracing** the words. Then **write** the words.

bear

ball

bee

Bobby

257

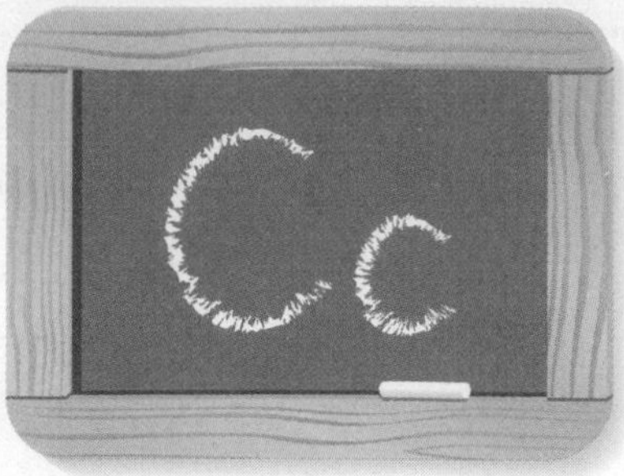

Name _____

Practice by **tracing** the letter. Then **write** the letter.

C — C — C — C — C — C

C — C — C — C — C — C

Name _____

Practice by **tracing** the words. Then **write** the words.

cats

cookies

cards

Chuck

Printing Letters and Words

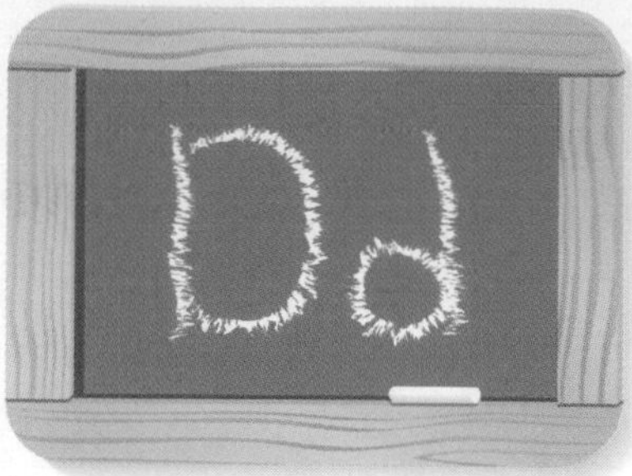

Name _____

Practice by **tracing** the letter. Then **write** the letter.

D — D — D — D — D — D

d — d — d — d — d — d

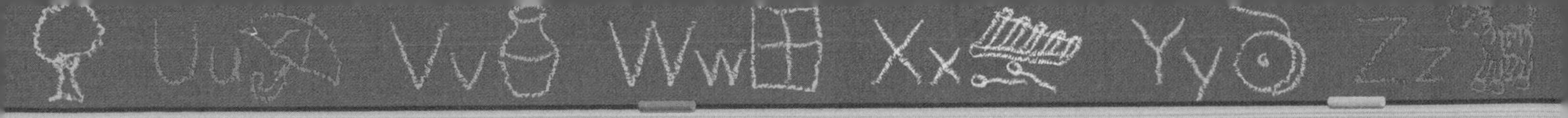

Name _____

Practice by **tracing** the words. Then **write** the words.

duck

dog

dance

Danny

Printing Letters and Words

Name _____

Practice by **tracing** the letter. Then **write** the letter.

Name _____

✏️ Practice by **tracing** the words. Then **write** the words.

elephant

egg

elbow

Ellie

263

Printing Letters and Words

Name _____

Practice by **tracing** the letter. Then **write** the letter.

Ff

Practice by **tracing** the words. Then **write** the words.

frog

fish

fox

Florida

Printing Letters and Words

Name _____

✏️ Practice by **tracing** the letter. Then **write** the letter.

G — G — G — G — G — G

g — g — g — g — g — g

Printing Letters and Words

Name _____

✏️ Practice by **tracing** the words. Then **write** the words.

giraffe

grass

glasses

Gretchen

Printing Letters and Words

Name _____

Practice by **tracing** the letter. Then **write** the letter.

Name _____

Practice by **tracing** the words. Then **write** the words.

hippo

hat

heart

Hannah

Printing Letters and Words

Aa Bb Cc Dd Ee Ff Gg

Name _____

Practice by **tracing** the letter. Then **write** the letter.

2 →
1
3 →

2 •
1

Printing Letters and Words

270

Name _____

Practice by **tracing** the words. Then **write** the words.

inchworm

iguana

igloo

Indiana

271

Printing Letters and Words

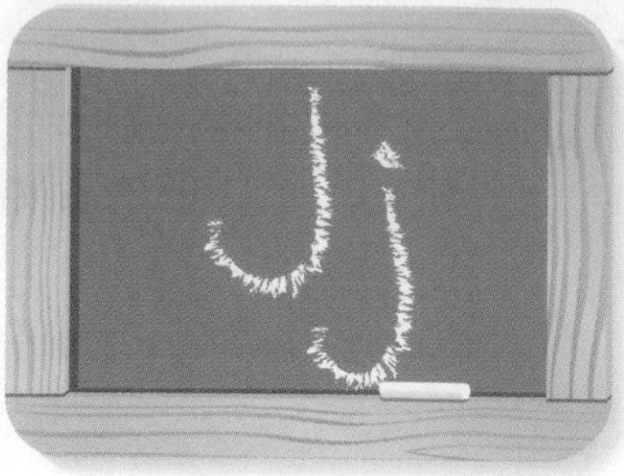

Name _____

✏ Practice by **tracing** the letter. Then **write** the letter.

J J J J J J

j j j j j j

Name _____

Practice by **tracing** the words. Then **write** the words.

jaguar

- - - - - - - - - - - - - - - -

jump

- - - - - - - - - - - - - - - -

jam

- - - - - - - - - - - - - - - -

June

- - - - - - - - - - - - - - - -

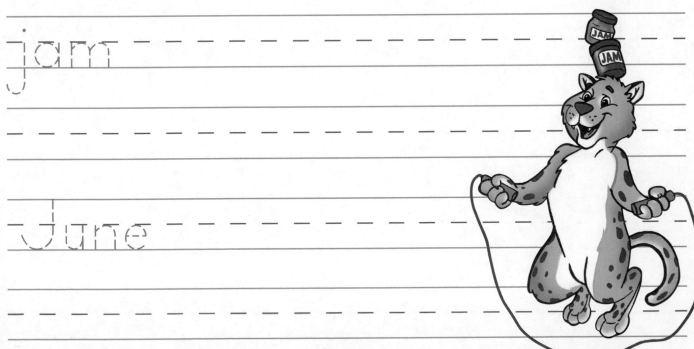

Printing Letters and Words

Name _____

✏️ Practice by **tracing** the letter. Then **write** the letter.

Name _____

✏ Practice by **tracing** the words. Then **write** the words.

kangaroo

kite

key

Kelsey

Printing Letters and Words

Name _____

Practice by **tracing** the letter. Then **write** the letter.

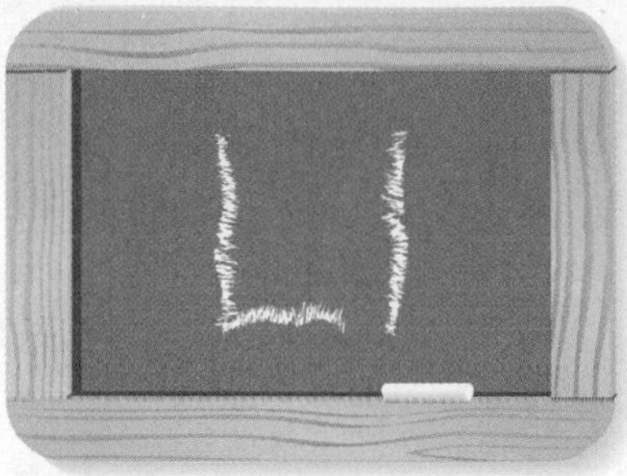

Name _____

✏️ Practice by **tracing** the words. Then **write** the words.

lion

lollipop

lick

Lori

Printing Letters and Words

Name _____

Practice by **tracing** the letter. Then **write** the letter.

M — M — M — M — M — M

m — m — m — m — m — m

Printing Letters and Words 278

Name _____

✏️ Practice by **tracing** the words. Then **write** the words.

monkey

mushroom

moon

Megan

279

Printing Letters and Words

Name _____

Practice by **tracing** the letter. Then **write** the letter.

N — N — N — N — N — N — N

n — n — n — n — n — n

Name _____

Practice by **tracing** the words. Then **write** the words.

newt

nest

note

Nebraska

281

Printing Letters and Words

Name _____

Practice by **tracing** the letter. Then **write** the letter.

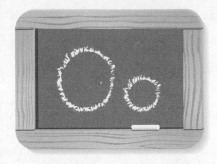

Name _____

✏️ Practice by **tracing** the words. Then **write** the words.

ostrich

octopus

olive

Olivia

Printing Letters and Words

Name _____

Practice by **tracing** the letter. Then **write** the letter.

P _ _ P _ _ P _ _ P _ _ P _ _ P

P _ _ P _ _ P _ _ P _ _ P _ _ P

Printing Letters and Words

284

Practice by **tracing** the words. Then **write** the words.

penguin

pizza

pencil

Paul

Printing Letters and Words

Practice by **tracing** the letter. Then **write** the letter.

Name _____

Practice by **tracing** the words. Then **write** the words.

quail

queen

quarter

Quincy

Printing Letters and Words

Name _____

Practice by **tracing** the letter. Then **write** the letter.

R - - R - - R - - R - - R - - R

r   r   r   r   r   r

Name _____

Practice by **tracing** the words. Then **write** the words.

rabbit

ribbon

race

Randy

Printing Letters and Words

Name _____

Ss

Practice by **tracing** the letter. Then **write** the letter.

S S S S S S S S S S S S

S S S S S S S S S S S S

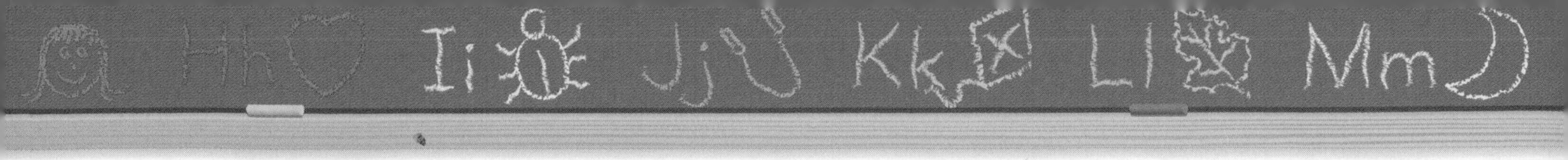

Name _____

Practice by **tracing** the words. Then **write** the words.

Ss

seat

sun

shell

Susan

Printing Letters and Words

Name _____

Practice by **tracing** the letter. Then **write** the letter.

Name _____

Practice by **tracing** the words. Then **write** the words.

turtle

tiger

tie

Tom

Printing Letters and Words

Aa Bb Cc Dd Ee Ff Gg

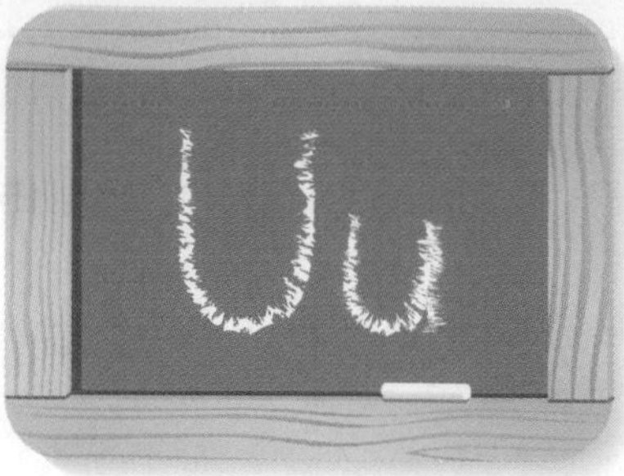

Name _____

Practice by **tracing** the letter. Then **write** the letter.

U U U U U U U

u u u u u u

Printing Letters and Words

294

Name _____

✏️ Practice by **tracing** the words. Then **write** the words.

umpire

umbrella

under

Uncle Bob

Printing Letters and Words

Name _____

Practice by **tracing** the letter. Then **write** the letter.

Name _____

Vv

✏️ Practice by **tracing** the words. Then **write** the words.

vulture

violin

vest

Vicki

Printing Letters and Words

Name _____

Practice by **tracing** the letter. Then **write** the letter.

Name _____

🖊 Practice by **tracing** the words. Then **write** the words.

whale

walrus

water

William

299

Printing Letters and Words

Name _____

Practice by **tracing** the letter. Then **write** the letter.

X - - X - - X - - X - - X - - X

X - - X - - X - - X - - X - - X

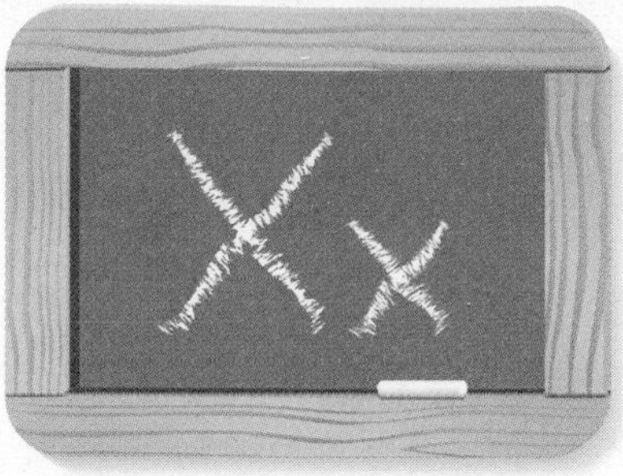

Name _____

✎ Practice by **tracing** the words. Then **write** the words.

xylophone

fox

mix

X ray

Printing Letters and Words

Name _____

✏️ Practice by **tracing** the letter. Then **write** the letter.

Name _____

Practice by **tracing** the words. Then **write** the words.

yak

yo-yo

yarn

Yvonne

303

Printing Letters and Words

Name _____

✏️ Practice by **tracing** the letter. Then **write** the letter.

Name _____

Practice by **tracing** the words. Then **write** the words.

zebra

zipper

zoo

Zack

ZOO

305

Printing Letters and Words

Name _____

GOOD JOB!

WELL DONE!

I can print alphabet letters!

Show off your printing by **writing** your name and age below. Then **color** the whole picture!

Name:_____

Age:_____

Date:_____

Printing Letters and Words

306

For Parents, Caregivers, and Educators

This section includes songs, rhymes, and activities that allow children to learn and reinforce the letters of the alphabet in creative and playful ways. Even very young children can participate in the songs, rhymes, and games, and become more familiar with the alphabet.

There are several activities for each letter of the alphabet. They feature a variety of curriculum areas such as art, language, math, science, music, movement, and learning games. Many of these activities can serve as springboards to other ideas; that is, you may think of another or better way of presenting a certain letter.

If some of the activities appear to be too juvenile for the children that you are working with, encourage them to lead a younger sibling or friend in the songs and verses. This will help reinforce the alphabet for the child leading the activities.

Although these songs, rhymes, and games are educational, they are also fun. Enjoy each activity with the children as you work with them to better learn and understand the alphabet.

Name _____

My A Book

Make a book for each child by stapling several sheets of white paper together with a construction paper cover. Print "My A Book" and the child's name on the front. Set out magazine pictures of things whose names begin with A, along with upper- and lowercase A's cut from ads or article titles. Let the children choose the pictures and letters they want and glue them onto their book pages. Later, arrange a time for the children to "read" their books to you.

A, A, What Can I Say?

A, A, what can I say?
Just what can I say about the letter A?

Airplane and *alligator* start with an A.
Acorn and *apple* begin the same way.

Anchor and *astronaut* start with A too,
As do *apron* and *acrobat*, to name just a few.

Abracadabra begins with an A.
It's a magical word that I like to say.

Ant and *ax* both start with A.
Let's hear it for A! Hip, hip, hurray!

Songs, Rhymes, and Activities

Letter Bb

Six Buzzing Bumblebees

Cut six ovals out of black felt. Glue yellow felt strips on the ovals to make simple felt bees. If desired, label each bee with a sticker *B* or a felt *B*. Place the bees on a flannel board. As you recite the poem below, remove the bees one at a time.

Six buzzing bumblebees
Flying around the hive,
One buzzes off
And that leaves five.

Five buzzing bumblebees
Flying near my door,
One buzzes off
And that leaves four.

Four buzzing bumblebees
Flying around a tree,
One buzzes off
And that leaves three.

Three buzzing bumblebees
In the sky so blue,
One buzzes off
And that leaves two.

Two buzzing bumblebees
Flying by the sun,
One buzzes off
And that leaves one.

One buzzing bumblebee
Looking for some fun,
It buzzes off
And that leaves none.

Name _____

Letter
C c

Clothes on the Clothesline

Cut clothes shapes out of construction paper. Print the letter *C* on most of the shapes and print other letters on the rest. Hang a clothesline between two chairs and set out a basket of clothespins. Remind the children that *clothes*, *clothesline*, and *clips* all begin with C. Let the children take turns sorting through the clothes shapes and clipping those that are marked with *C* to the clothesline.

C Song

Sung to: "Skip to My Lou"

Carrots, castles, candy canes,
Cucumbers and clouds with rain,
Cats and cookies, crayons too.
I think *C* is cool. Don't you?

311

Songs, Rhymes, and Activities

Name _____

Letter Dd

Dot *D*'s

Cut large letter *D* shapes out of heavy paper. Let the children decorate their letters by attaching different colored self-stick dots. Or use a hole punch to punch small circles out of construction paper. Remind the children that the word *dot* begins with *d*. Have the children glue the circle "dots" on their *D* shapes.

Put Some Doughnuts on the Dish

Sung to: "If You're Happy and You Know It"

Put some doughnuts on the dish, on the dish,
Put some doughnuts on the dish, on the dish.
Put some doughnuts on the dish,
Put as many as you wish.
Then say, "*D* is for the doughnuts on the dish."

Repeat, substituting other words that begin with *d* for the word *doughnuts*.

Songs, Rhymes, and Activities

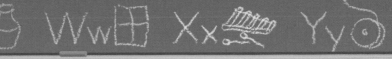

Name _____

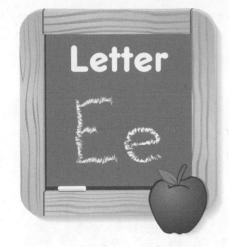

Elephants Balancing

Arrange a long piece of string on the floor in a wide circle. Have the children line up by the circle and pretend to be elephants. Recite the rhyme below and let the first child in line start walking around on the string. Then have the second child start walking on the string as you repeat the rhyme, this time beginning with the words "Two little elephants balancing." Continue in the same manner until all the children are walking on the string. Then change the last line of the poem to read: "Now, no more elephants."

One little elephant balancing,
Step by step on a piece of string.
Oh, my—what a stunt!
Now, here comes another elephant.

E, E, What Do You See?

Sung to: "Skip to My Lou"

E, E, What do you see?
What do you see that starts with *E*?
I see an elf, that's what I see.
Hip, hip, hurray for *E*!

Repeat, substituting other words that start with *e* for the word *elf*. Set out some objects to help the children, if you wish: an egg, a stuffed elephant, an easel, an envelope, and an eraser, or pictures of an elbow, an ear, an eye, an elevator, an emergency squad, a railroad engineer, an exit sign, and any other *e* words you can think of.

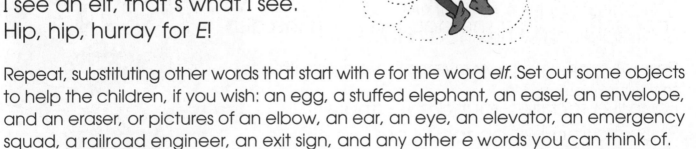

Songs, Rhymes, and Activities

Letter Ff

Fingerpainted Fans

Give each child a paper plate to use for the top part of a fan. Let the children fingerpaint on their plates, using any color(s) they wish. Allow the plates to dry on a flat surface. Make a handle for each fan by gluing two tongue depressors together and slipping the edge of the paper plate between them. When the glue has dried, have the children print the letters *Ff* on each fan. Then let the children have fun fanning their faces with their fingerpainted fans.

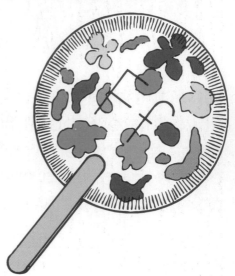

Found an *F*

Place items whose names begin with *f* on the floor. Some examples of things you might use are flower, feather, fork, fan, toy frog, toy fish, toy fence, flag, flute, football, fur. Have the children sit in a circle around the items. Let one child begin by choosing an item, holding it up, and naming it. Then sing the song below, substituting the name of the item for *feather* and the child's name for *Jamie*. Continue until each child has had a turn.

Sung to: "Found a Peanut"

Found a feather, found a feather,
Found a feather on the floor.
Jamie just now found a feather
Found a feather on the floor.

Name _____

Creating Green

Place small amounts of yellow and blue fingerpaint inside a recloseable plastic sandwich bag. Have the children sit in a circle. Pass the bag around and let each child rub it gently in his or her hands. When the bag gets back to you, hold it up and let the children observe the new color they created. Announce "*G* is for green!"

G Song

Sung to: "Twinkle, Twinkle, Little Star"

When I look around I see
Many things that start with G.
I see *grass* and *girls* galore,
I see *gloves* and so much more.
Won't you look around with me
And sing for things that start with G?

Have the children sit in a circle on the floor. Repeat, substituting other words that begin with *g* for the words *grass*, *girls*, and *gloves*. Have pictures of *g* items such as *gate*, *grasshopper*, *gift*, *gum*, *glass*, *garden*, *garage*, *gas pump*, *glitter*, *glue*, *globe*, *goggles*, and *golf club* in the middle of the circle to give children ideas for other pictures whose names begin with *g*.

Letter Hh

H's in the House

Decorate a box to look like a house and print the letters *Hh* for *house* on the front. Cut index cards in half. Print *Hh* on most of the cards and print other letters on the rest. Let the children take turns sorting through the cards and placing those that are marked with *Hh* inside the house.

I Am a Housepainter

Sung to: "Hokey-Pokey"

I dip my paintbrush in,
I take my paintbrush out,
I dip my paintbrush in,
Then I brush it on a house.
I am a housepainter,
And I paint inside and out.
That's what my job's about.

Letter Ii

Inkblots

Give each child a sheet of white construction paper. Let the children squeeze drops of colored ink or food coloring (to resemble ink) on their papers. Help them fold their papers in half. Have them gently rub across their papers and then unfold them to reveal the inkblot designs they created. Encourage the children to tell what they think their inkblots look like. Then cut out the designs and use them to make a bulletin board display titled "*I* Is for *Inkblots*."

I Is Such a Simple Letter

Sung to: "Twinkle, Twinkle, Little Star"

I is such a simple letter,
There's no other that I like better.
I stands for me when I want it to,
I is for *ink* and for *ice cream* too.
I is such a simple letter,
There's no other that I like better.

Repeat, substituting other words that begin with *i* for the words *ink* and *ice cream*.

Letter J

Jewelry J's

Give each child a 6-inch-tall *J* shape cut from posterboard. Have the children decorate their letters by gluing on such materials as glitter, small beads, sequins, or foil scraps. Punch holes in the tops of the letter shapes. Then tie on loops of yarn or colored cord and let the children wear their "jewelry *J*'s" as necklaces.

A Journey to Japan

I am taking a journey to Japan,
My jet is leaving in June.
I am packing up my *J* things,
You'd think I was off to the moon.

I am taking a jack-o'-lantern
And plenty of juice and Jell-O.
Of course, I will take my jewelry
And my jacket that's sort of yellow.

I am planning to take my jellyfish,
Who speaks perfect Japanese.
He taught me how to jitterbug,
Jeepers, that jars the knees!

I packed a jigsaw puzzle
And a book about how to juggle.
I didn't forget my jack rabbit,
The bed toy I love to snuggle.

Now I'll just pack my jump rope
And a jar of jam, if I can.
Then I think I'll have all my *J* things
For my journey to Japan.

Read the rhyme once through to the children. Then repeat the rhyme slowly and have children raise their hands as they hear a *j* word. Have them name the word that begins with *j*.

Letter Kk

Kangaroo Pouch Game

Draw a large picture of a kangaroo on a sheet of posterboard. Cut a pocket shape from fabric and staple it to the kangaroo picture for a pouch. Title the picture "*K* Is for *Kangaroo*" and hang it on a wall at the children's eye level. Cut several pictures from magazines, most of them of objects that begin with *k*, and place them facedown on a desk or table. Have children come to the desk or table one at a time and choose a picture. If the picture name begins with *k*, he or she can put the picture in the kangaroo's pouch. If the picture name begins with another letter, have the child place it in a separate pile.

We Say *K*'s OK

Sung to: "Old MacDonald Had a Farm"

There is a letter we all know,
And its name is *K*.
K is a letter that we like.
We say *K*'s OK.
K is for *king*, *K* is for *key*,
K is for all the *kites* we see.
There is a letter we all know,
And its name is *K*.

Repeat, substituting other words that begin with *k* for the words *king*, *key*, and *kites*.

Songs, Rhymes, and Activities

Name _____

I'm a Lion

Sung to: "Three Blind Mice"

I'm a lion, I'm a lion,
Hear me roar, hear me roar.
I love to sleep out in the sun,
And chase other animals just for fun.
In all the jungle I'm Number One.
I'm a lion.

Ask children to substitute other animal names
that begin with the letter *l* and make appropriate
substitutions in the song and sing it with the new
words. For instance, they might choose *lamb*,
baaa, and *barnyard*.

Leg Twist

Print large upper- and lowercase
Ll's on a long piece of butcher
paper, spacing them out evenly.
Ask one child to place one foot
on an uppercase *L* and the other
foot on a lowercase *l*. Have the first
child remain standing in place as a second
child locates an upper- and lowercase *Ll* to stand
on. Continue until all the children are standing on the butcher paper.
The more children that are involved in the game, the more giggles
and unusual positions there will be.

Name _____

Letter Mm

Musical Chairs

Place a chair for each child in a circle, facing out. Tape a picture whose name begins with *m* on the backs of most of the chairs. On the remaining chairs, tape a picture whose name begins with another letter. Start the music while the children walk around the chairs. When the music stops, children should try to find a chair with a picture whose name begins with *m*. Those left standing or sitting in chairs with pictures whose names begin with another letter must leave the game. Make sure that there is always at least one chair whose picture names an object that begins with a letter other than *m*. Continue play until the last child is seated in a chair that names an object that begins with *m*.

The M's Are Marching

Sung to: "When Johnny Comes Marching Home"

The *M*'s are marching round the room, hurray, hurray!
The *M*'s are marching round the room in a big parade.
A *monkey*, a *mouse*, a *mitten*, and *more*,
All are marching round the floor.
Oh, we're all so glad that they could come today!

Let three children at a time hold items that begin with *m* as you sing and march around in a circle. Substitute the names of the items for the words *monkey*, *mouse*, and *mitten*.

Songs, Rhymes, and Activities

Newspaper *N*'s

Collect the comics section from newspapers. Give each child one comics page and a felt-tip marker. Have the children search for *N* or *n* on their newspaper pages and circle them with their felt-tip markers.

Remind the children that the word *newspaper* begins with *n*. After all the children have finished, have them count their *N*'s and *n*'s and see who has the most.

N Song

Sung to: "Ten Little Indians"

N is for *nine* and *N* is for *noodles*,
N is for *nine* and *N* is for *noodles*,
N is for *nine* and *N* is for *noodles*.
Let's count *nine noodles* now.

One little, two little, three little *noodles*,
  (Count out noodles one at a time.)
Four little, five little, six little *noodles*,
Seven little, eight little, *nine* little *noodles*.
Nine little *noodles* now.

Continue with similar verses, substituting such objects as *napkins*, *nickels*, or *nuts* for *noodles*.

Name _____

O Chains

Cut construction paper into 1- by 10-inch strips. Place the strips in a box and set out glue. Let the children use the paper strips to make chains of O's. If desired, hook the chains together as they are completed and hang them around the room.

Printing O's

Pour different colors of tempera paint into shallow containers. Set out construction paper and objects with round open ends, such as cardboard toilet tissue tubes, drinking straws, margarine tubs, and plastic bottles. Invite the children to print O's of various colors and sizes by dipping the open ends of the objects into the paint and pressing them onto their papers. Encourage them to make a colorful design on their papers.

Songs, Rhymes, and Activities

Name _____

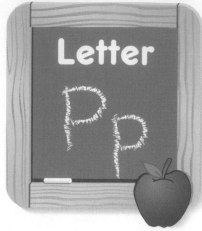

Letter Pp

Paula Had a Party

Paula had a *party*, and I think you'll agree
That a lot of attention was paid to *P*.

Poodles and *polar* bears *paraded* by.
Pigeons and *parakeets* came to fly.

Penguins splashed around
in *Paula's pool*.
People drank *purple* juice
just to keep cool.

Peaches and *pears* were
served on *plates*.
The *peanuts* and *popcorn*
tasted just great.

Panda played the *piano*,
ever so *proud*,
Till *Paula* shouted, "You're
playing too loud!"

Then *Paula* looked around,
her *place* was a mess.
She was tired of *P*, she needed a rest.

"*Please* leave my *party*!" *Paula* said.
Then *Paula* turned around and went to bed.

Read the poem through one time. Then read it again slowly, asking the children to raise their hands every time they hear a word that begins with the letter *p*. Ask them to name the *p* word.

Letter

Name _____

Q Is for *Quilt*

Give each child a 9-inch square of construction paper that has been creased diagonally both ways. Cut or have the children cut diamond shapes from aluminum foil and colorful paper scraps. Let the children glue the diamond shapes on their squares in patterns, using the creases on their squares as guidelines. Arrange the squares in a rectangular shape on the floor and tape them all together to make a quilt. Display the quilt on a wall or a bulletin board and title it "*Q* Is for *Quilt.*"

I Like Q

Sung to: "Twinkle, Twinkle, Little Star"

Q is for *queen* with a crown on
 her head,
Q is for *quilt* that covers my bed.
Q is for *questions* I like asking,
Q is for ducklings'
 quack-quack-quacking.
Q is for *quarter* and *quick* and *quill,*
I like *Q* and I always will.

325

Letter Rr

Rock Matching Game

Collect five pairs of rocks ranging in size from small to large. Paint the rocks and allow them to dry. Group the rocks into pairs of matching sizes. Print an uppercase R on one of the rocks in each pair and a lowercase r on the other. Then mix up the rocks and let the children take turns finding the matching pairs.

Round Go the R's

Sung to: "Ten Little Indians"

Round and round and round go the R's,
Round and round and round go the R's,
Round and round and round go the R's.
Round and round the ring.

Round goes a rock and a rope and a ruler,
Round goes a rock and a rope and a ruler,
Round goes a rock and a rope and a ruler,
Round and round the ring.

Let three children at a time hold *R* items as they sing and walk around in a circle. Substitute the names of the items for the words *rock, rope,* and *ruler.*

Name _____

Sandy Snakes

Have the children brush glue onto sheets of paper to create fat snakes that look like *S*'s. You may wish to demonstrate the *S* shape on the board.

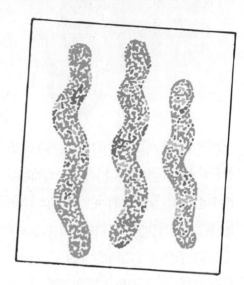

Have them sprinkle sand on the wet glue and then tap off the excess sand over a trash can. After the glue has dried, encourage the children to feel their sandy snakes with their hands.

S Movement Game

Recite the poem below and have the children act out the movements described.

Stand in a circle, *stoop* down low,
Now *stand* up *straight* and tall.
Stamp, stamp, stamp your feet,
Now quietly curl up *small*.

Swing, swing, swing your arms,
Stretch, stretch your *spines*.
Sway, sway, swing, and *sway*,
Now *smile*—you're looking fine!

After the children have completed the activity once, ask them what movements begin with the letter *s*.

Name _____

Letter T t

Tissue Triangle Art

Cut or have the children cut triangles out of different colors of tissue paper. Set out brushes and diluted glue. Give each child a piece of waxed paper. Have the children brush the glue onto their papers and place the triangles on top of the glue. Encourage them to work on small areas at a time and to overlap their triangles to create new colors. For a shiny effect, brush more glue over the children's papers after they have finished. Attach construction paper frames. Then punch a hole in one corner of each frame and hang the papers from the ceiling or on a bulletin board.

Tap Your *Toe* for *T*

Sung to: "Row, Row, Row Your Boat"

Tap, tap, tap your *toe*,
Tap your *toe* for *T*.
Tap for *train* and *turkey* and *toy*,
Tap, tap, one, two, three.

Repeat, substituting other words that begin with *t* for the words *train, turkey,* and *toy*.

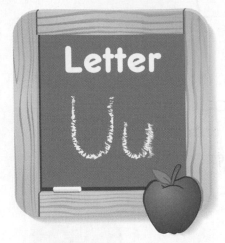

Letter Uu

Name _____

Umbrella Color Game

Cut one umbrella shape each from the following colors of felt: green, red, purple, blue, yellow, and orange. Hand one umbrella shape a piece to six students. (You may wish to read the poem more than once to allow every student to have one umbrella shape.) As you read the poem below, let the child with the appropriate umbrella place the umbrella on a flannelboard. Remind the children that the word *umbrella* begins with the letter *u*.

We keep our umbrellas not far away,
Reading and waiting for a rainy day.

Here is a green one to keep me dry
When I open it up and hold it high.

Have you seen the umbrella that's ruby red?
It looks so regal held over my head.

The rain can get heavy, oh me, oh my,
But the purple umbrella will keep me dry.

I love the umbrella of sweet sky blue.
It's big enough for both me and you.

The yellow umbrella is bright like the sun.
Jumping puddles with it is ever so fun.

The orange umbrella is saved for showers,
The kind of rain that wakes up the flowers.

Our umbrellas are fun and so nice to see.
Just look at them all; I'm sure you'll agree.

Songs, Rhymes, and Activities

Letter Vv

Volcano Fun

Make a "volcano" by placing a small paper cup upright in a pie pan and forming a mountain around it with clay or playdough. Inside the cup place a tablespoon of baking soda.

Let the children take turns adding tablespoons of vinegar to the cup and observing as the volcano "erupts." Remind the children that the words *volcano* and *vinegar* begin with *v*.

I Love to Make the Letter V

Sung to: "Pop! Goes the Weasel"

I love to make the letter *V*
For everyone to see.
(Form *V* with two fingers.)
V is for *vinegar*, *V* is for *van*,
And *V* is for *victory*!

Repeat, substituting other words that begin with *v* for the words *vinegar* and *van*. (You may wish to keep *victory* in the last line of the song for rhyming purposes.)

Letter Ww

Welcome, Little W

Sung to: "Twinkle, Twinkle, Little Star"

Welcome, little *W*,
We like you, we really do.
Waffles that we love to eat,
Watermelons, oh, so sweet.
W, we'll wave today,
When we see you come our way.

Welcome, little *W*,
We like you, we really do.
Worms and *wagons* here and there,
Walls and *windows* everywhere.
W, we'll wave today,
When we see you come our way.

Continue with similar verses, substituting other words that begin with *w* for the words *worms*, *wagons*, *walls*, and *windows*.

Wallpaper W's

Cut a large letter *W* shape for each child out of heavy paper. Set out glue and wallpaper samples. Remind the children that *wallpaper* begins with *w*. Let the children tear the wallpaper into small pieces and glue them all over their letters.

Songs, Rhymes, and Activities

Name _____

Letter
X x

X Marks the Spot

Tape a large poster board *X* to the floor (or make an *X* with masking tape). Print *X*'s and other letters on Post-it® notes and stick them on objects around the room. Let the children walk around and search for the *X* notes. Whenever a child finds one, have him or her remove it and then stick it to the center of the large *X* on the floor. Continue until each child has found at least one *X* note.

Extension: Follow up by playing an "*X* Marks the Spot" game. Attach a squeaky toy to the center of the *X* on the floor. Then let the children take turns trying to toss a beanbag onto the center of the *X* to make the toy squeak.

X's Mean Kisses

Sung to: "Skip to My Lou"

X's mean kisses I like a lot,
X is for *X ray* and "*X* marks the spot."
X is for *xylophone* I like to play,
X is quite extra-special, I'd say.

Young Yolanda

Bring in a yo-yo and demonstrate how to use it. You may wish to pass the yo-yo around and have the children try using it. Then read the poem below, encouraging the children to join in on the repeated verses. As they do so, have them move one arm up and down like a yo-yo. You may wish to pass the yo-yo around and have those who want to, work the yo-yo on the chorus "That's the way the yo-yo goes."

Young Yolanda rides a *yak*,
Sitting proudly on its back.

High, low—High, low.
That the way the yo-yo goes.

Young Yolanda sails a *yacht*,
Especially when it's very hot.

High, low—High, low.
That's the way the yo-yo goes.

Young Yolanda does her *yoga*
In a sunny *yellow* toga.

High, low—High, low.
That's the way the yo-yo goes.

Young Yolanda just loves *yams*,
Served up nicely with canned hams.

High, low—High, low.
That's the way the yo-yo goes.

Yolanda *yodels* in her *yard*.
That Yolanda's such a card!

High, low—High, low.
That's the way the yo-yo goes.

Yolanda says that *yogurt's yummy*,
Good and healthy in your tummy.

High, low—High, low.
That's the way the yo-yo goes.

After you've read through the poem once, read it a second time slowly and have the children tell you each time you name a word that begins with *y* (other than the repeated chorus). Have them name the word that begins with *y*.

Songs, Rhymes, and Activities

Name _____

Zither Fun

Make a "zither" for the children to play with to introduce the sound of z. Pound nails at opposite ends of a sturdy board and stretch rubber bands from nail to nail as shown in the illustration. Print the letters Zz on the side of your zither to show that *zither* begins with z. Have the children take turns plucking it as the class sings favorite songs.

Five Little Zinnias

Make five zinnia shapes out of felt and print Z's in the centers. Place the shapes on a flannelboard. Let the children take turns "picking" the zinnias as you read the poem below.

Five little zinnias,
Growing outside my door.
I picked one for Grandma,
Now there are four.

Four little zinnias,
The prettiest I've seen.
I picked one for Grandpa,
Now there are three.

Three little zinnias,
Just a lovely few.
I picked one for Mommy,
Now there are two.

Two little zinnias,
Reaching for the sun.
I picked one for Daddy,
Now there is one.

One little zinnia.
A colorful little hero.
I picked it just for you,
Now there are zero.

CONGRATULATIONS!
You know your Alphabet!

Color this ribbon your favorite colors. Cut it out and wear it or hang it up for everyone to see!

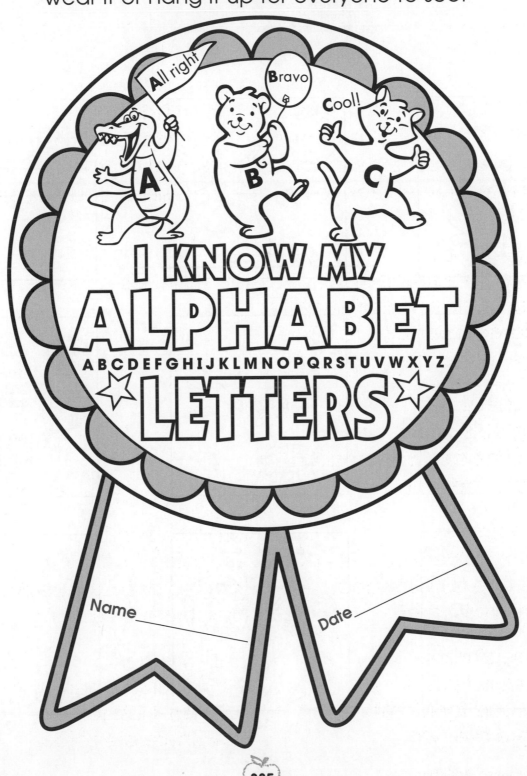

Answer Key

7

Apple alligator angel bat
Amy dance Andy at
ambulance draw teacher nap

8

A is for **a**pple.

A is for **a**ngel.

A is for **a**nt.

9

11

Bill brown doll Bonnie
boy baby balloon pig
bat book butter band

BOOK

12

B is for **b**uttons.

B is for **b**at.

B is for **b**ug.

13

14

16

Cat Casey ran can
cow corn cup Carol
hand wall crack car

17

C is for **c**ow.

C is for **c**up.

C is for **c**at.

18

19

doll Darcy desk big
door David jump dog
pig Daddy duck Debbie

21

D is for **d**og.

D is for **d**rum.

D is for **d**uck.

22

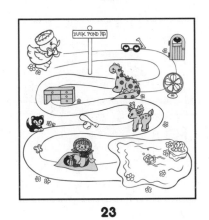

23

24

car Elizabeth his moon
dog house earth Eric
ball of cat envelope

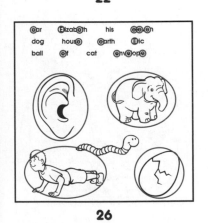

26

E is for **e**nvelope.

E is for **e**ggs.

E is for **e**lephant.

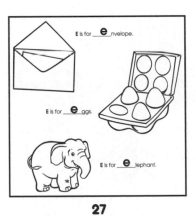

27

28

fire Faye took fork
table Fred car farm
Father ten four fish

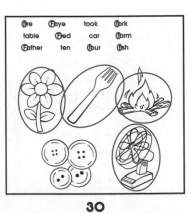

30

F is for **f**rog.

F is for **f**ish.

F is for **f**an.

31

32

337

Answer Key

33

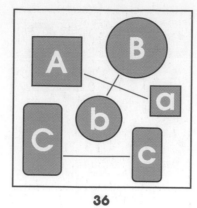

36

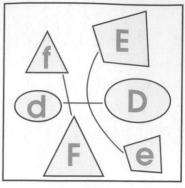

37

38

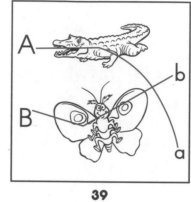

39

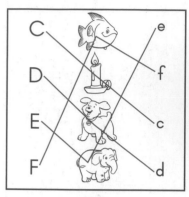

40

42

43

44

45

47

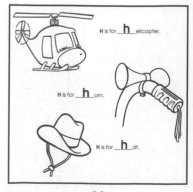

48

Answer Key

338

49

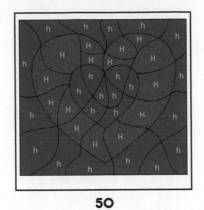

50

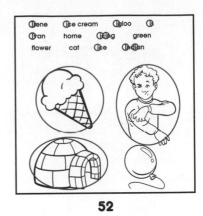

Irene Ice cream Igloo I
Ivan home Iing green
flower cat Ice Iian

52

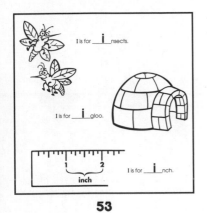

I is for __i__nsects.

I is for __i__gloo.

I is for __i__nch.

inch 1 2

53

54

Jamal Jump go Jennifer
took Jasmine Jug Jar
Joke Jack leaf Jelly

JAR

56

J is for __j__ump rope.

J is for __j__ar of __j__am.

Jam

J is for __j__ug.

57

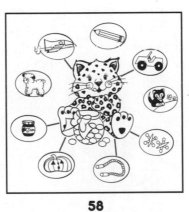

58

59

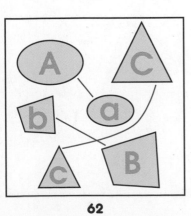

A C
b a
c B

62

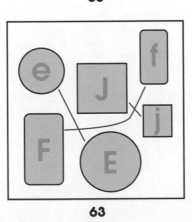

e f
J
j
F E

63

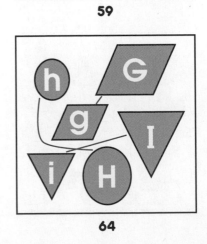

h G
g
i H I

64

Answer Key

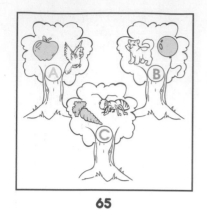

65

66

68

69

70

71

73

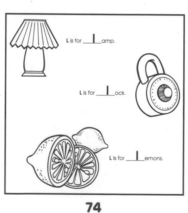

74

75

76

78

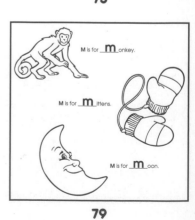

79

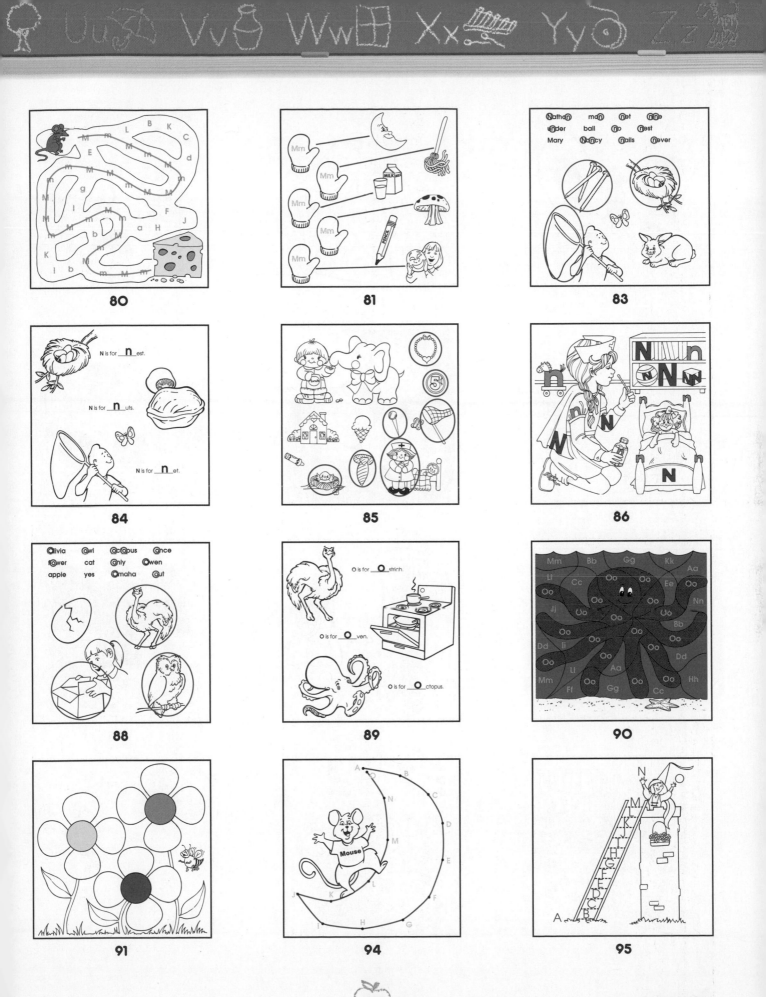

80

81

83

84

85

86

88

89

90

91

94

95

Answer Key

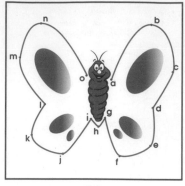

96

97

99

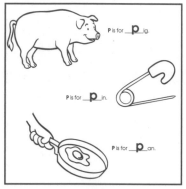

100

101

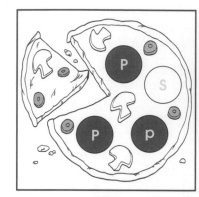

102

104

105

106

107

109

110

Answer Key

 342

111

112

114

115

116

117

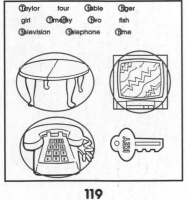

119

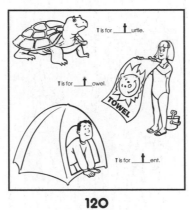

120

121

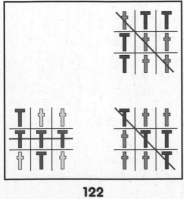

122

125

126

343

128

129

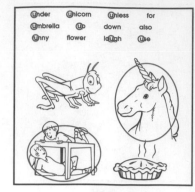

133

134

135

137

138

139

140

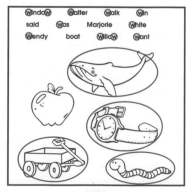

142

143

144

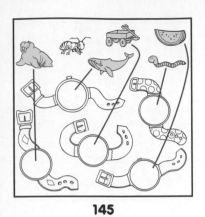

145

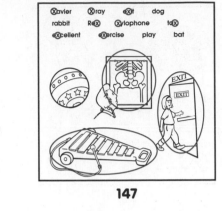

147

X is for __X__ ray.

X is in E __X__ it.

X is for __X__ ylophone.

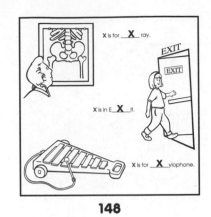

148

149

Yarn Yo Yo Yard Yuri
Yvonne Yes Yoke watch
vine Yesterday Yellow us

151

Y is for __y__ o-yo.

Y is for __y__ arn.

Y is for __y__ ogurt.

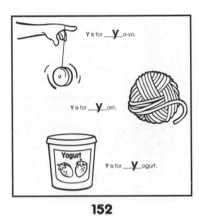

152

153

154

Zipper Zebra last Zig Zag
jazz Zelda Zoom Zero
frog Zone Pzard Zoo

156

Z is for __Z__ ipper.

Z is for __Z__ ig-zag.

Z is for __Z__ ebra.

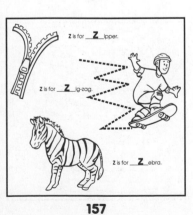

157

158

162

345

Answer Key

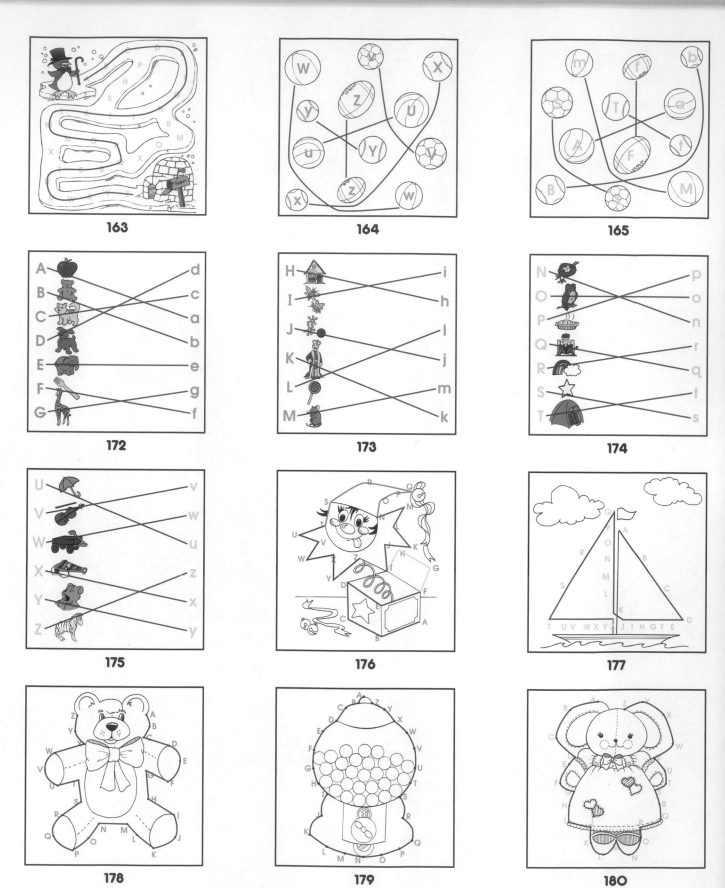

181

182

184

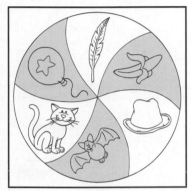

185

186

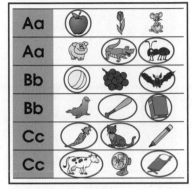

187

188

189

190

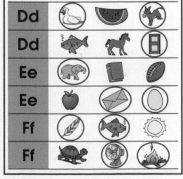

191

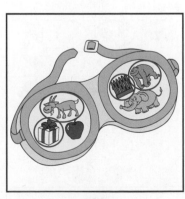

192

193

347 with apple, Answer Key

Answer Key

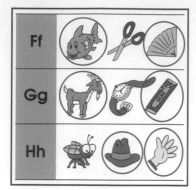

194

195

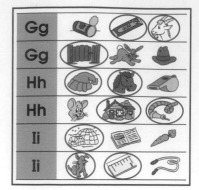

196

What is Jamie wearing? **jeans**

197

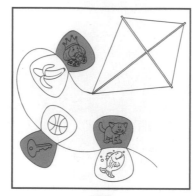

198

199

200

201

202

203

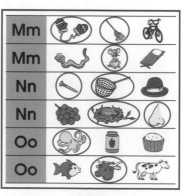

204

205

Answer Key

348

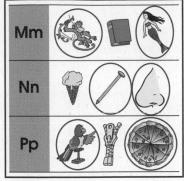

206

207

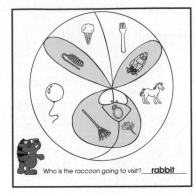

Who is the raccoon going to visit? __rabbit__

208

209

210

211

212

213

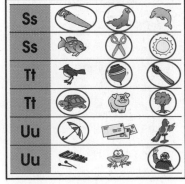

214

BE
MINE

215

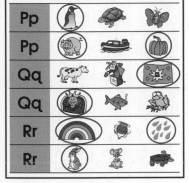

216

217

Answer Key

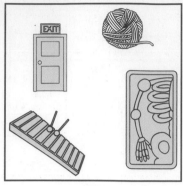

218

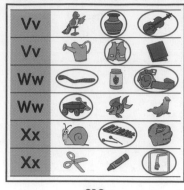

219

220

221

222

223

224

225

226

227

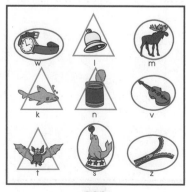

228

229

230

231

232

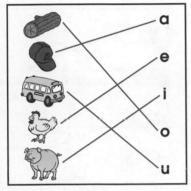

233

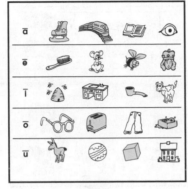

234

235

236

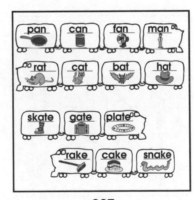

237

238

239

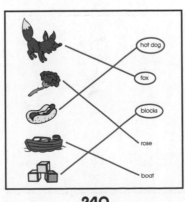

240

241

Answer Key

242

c **a** t   b **i** k e

sm **o** k **e**   tr **ee**

c **u** b   p **i** n

m **o** m   b **i** b

d **a** d   d **u** ck

244

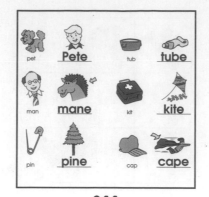

pet   **Pete**   tub   **tube**

man   **mane**   kit   **kite**

pin   **pine**   cap   **cape**

245

bl fl cl   cl fl (gl)   (fl) bl pl

fl (cl) gl   (pl) gl cl   gl fl (sl)

(gl) fl cl   sl (fl) cl   (cl) gl sl

246

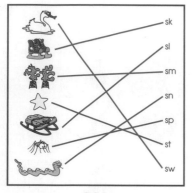

sk · sl · sm · sn · sp · st · sw

247

be **lt**   ra **ft**   sa **lt**   qui **lt**   le **ft**

248

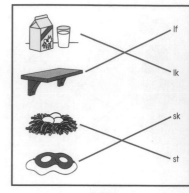

lf · lk · sk · st

249

250

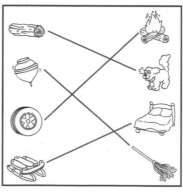

251

Example:

soap / rope   X   book / hook

X old rock   cat / hat   yellow black X

X it   rock / sock   rat / flat

X good rose   you / to   most X

old / sold   sale / whale   X wood letter

252